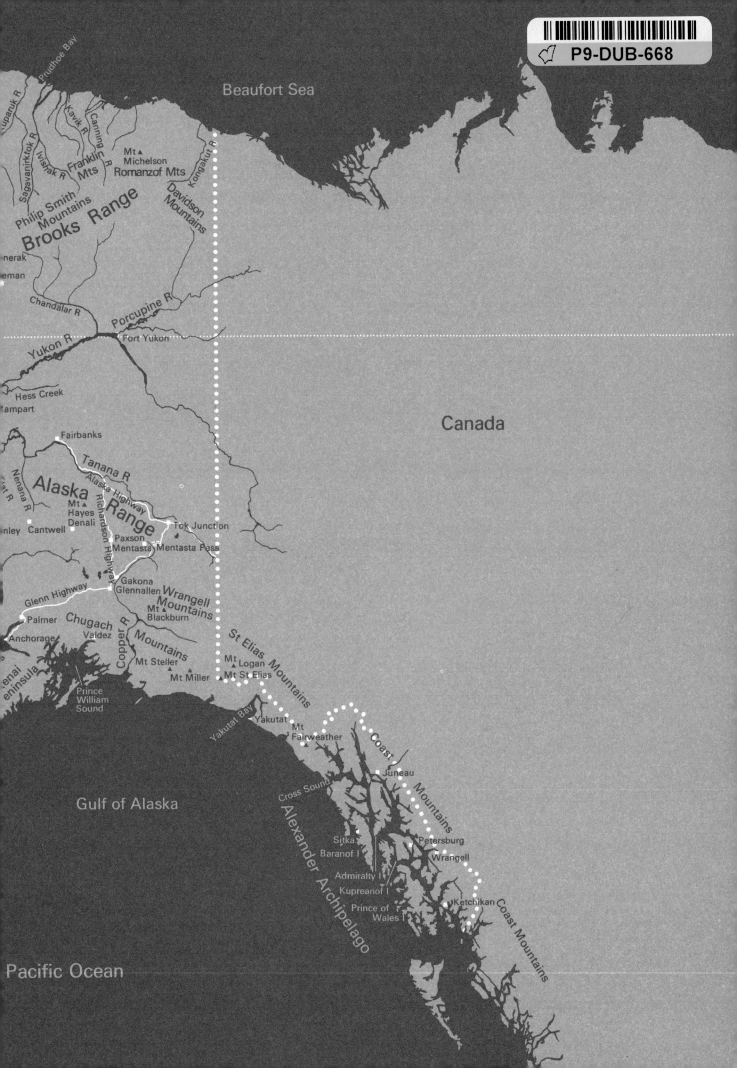

# Alaska
## and its wildlife

# Alaska
## and its wildlife

### Bryan L. Sage

A Studio Book

The Viking Press · New York

# Contents

This book is dedicated to my wife and daughter who have enjoyed the wilderness experience in Alaska.

TO read Bryan Sage's manuscript has not been undiluted pleasure for me. This statement is a measure of his literary skill which consists of a sensitive mind recounting experiences and observations without the slightest attempt at what is called fine writing. Bryan Sage gives us a plain tale of a country which is unsurpassed in our present world for scenery, splendour at its most terrible and arrays of wild life, whether they be of white whales, emperor geese, white Dall sheep or the great brown bears we call grizzlies. The reason for my melancholy is that I was afar in that great land of Alaska twenty years ago; Bryan Sage has brought it all back, the wonder of that first encounter, and the love I have for the place which has welled up in subsequent visits. It is bitter-sweet melancholy which I have welcomed.

Here is a naturalist of the old school who has as much delight in a flower or a butterfly as with the majesty of sandhill cranes soaring or caribou on migration. He is not writing a professional account of some scientific expedition but communicating his joy in observation; nothing is too small for his accurate, seeing eye. I myself walked many miles alone and I know that Bryan Sage has done so too because many of his thoughts are those which come to a man only when he is alone and utterly receptive of his surroundings.

Yet this man was in Alaska on a very material errand, trying to assess the ecological consequences of running an oil pipeline for 800 miles across Alaska between the Arctic and the Pacific Oceans. Some of us might well wish that oil had not been discovered on the Arctic slope but the point is that it has. The great find at Prudhoe Bay is a shock and a hurt to many of us. What are we going to do about it?

There are the quick-buck men who care nothing for wildlife or scenery or the integrity of the permafrost, but the major oil companies are not of this breed. As I see it, immense preparatory care is being taken, though obviously the Arctic slope is not going to be inviolate any more. The delay imposed by the United States Department of the Interior withholding permission for three years for construction of the pipeline will have done nothing but good. Survey will have been the surer and the wild enthusiasm reminiscent of a gold rush will have had time to cool down.

There are splendid biologists, geologists and geophysicists in Alaska. Their scientific response to the challenge of oil discovery has been admirable, as shown in numerous papers which have pruned much of the wild euphoria of those wishing to exploit regardless of consequences to the great land. If oil is to bring wealth to Alaska, let that wealth make sure of the conservation of much of Alaska in a way that would have been almost impossible without such wealth. The far future of Alaska will depend more on her preservation of wilderness areas than on oil, for the oil is finite in quantity and the evolution of the human species in an increasingly technological world is going to be towards a passionate appreciation of wilderness.

The discovery of oil, wisely managed, can be an event of opportunity to conserve. It is for Alaska to make it so and, as I see it, this oil-company ecologist who has written this book will be one who has done his best to conserve, in company with those other good scientists in Alaska. His book rings true.

*Frank Fraser Darling.*

5

# Introduction

THIS book is about Alaska as seen through the eyes of an Englishman. It deals not with politics or economics but with the wilderness and wildlife. To Americans, Alaska is the last great wilderness and the last frontier. If it fascinates the American and leaves a deep impression upon him, then it is not hard to imagine the effect it has on someone from the tame and gentle landscape of southern England with its dense population. Alaska impressed me in many ways, but the most lasting impressions were those of the wild and magnificent landscape, the beautiful wild flowers of the tundra and the abundant and varied wildlife.

I first went to Alaska early in 1969 when, as an ecologist with the British Petroleum Company, who have a large stake in Alaskan oil, I was sent out to look at the conservation and environmental problems associated with the proposed trans-Alaska crude oil pipeline from the Arctic coast southwards for nearly 800 miles to Valdez on the Gulf of Alaska. I continued my studies throughout 1970 and returned to Alaska again in 1971, this time to participate in the making of a film on the wildlife. In the course of my duties I travelled widely in the state by air, road, canoe and on foot. I saw many wonderful sights and made many fine friends. Are there friendlier people anywhere else in the world? I doubt it. The idea of writing a book, which first came to me in the winter of 1969, blossomed into a fixed intention in the summer of 1970 when, accompanied by Pete Martin of Anchorage, I back-packed from the watershed of the Brooks Range northwards towards the Arctic Ocean. We travelled well over a hundred miles down the valleys of the Atigun and Sagavanirktok Rivers, with many side excursions into other valleys. At the end of the trip I felt that I had a moral obligation to commit to paper my experiences in and feelings about the Alaskan wilderness.

There is a deeply entrenched notion in many quarters that oilmen are inherently 'hard-nosed' and see only the figures on the balance sheet. This is not entirely true. I have heard roughnecks on drilling rigs on the Arctic Slope wax very poetical about the beauties of that remote area, and not only when the midnight sun was shining! In the summer of 1971 certain biologists were studying whistling swans on the Arctic Slope where, it so happens, a pair were nesting close to the BP base camp. When it became known among the drillers and others that these studies involved the capture and marking of the swans, a notice appeared on the camp information board outlining dire threats to any scientist disturbing this particular pair of swans.

I have had the good fortune to have travelled widely in the world, but can think of nowhere, not even the deserts of the Middle East and North Africa, that has invoked as lasting an emotional response within me as has Alaska. In terms of scenery there is of course no comparison: Alaska is unique. I really have only one regret and that is that I did not see Alaska many years earlier, when it was even more remote and undisturbed than is the case now. Alaska has left an indelible impression on many past wanderers, as evidenced by the writings of men such as Vilhjalmur Stefansson, Robert Marshall and Adolph Murie. Well over eighty years ago John Muir wrote 'To the lover of pure wilderness, Alaska is one of the most wonderful countries in the world'. It still is.

I think it is on the Arctic Slope and in the northern foothills of the Brooks Range that one experiences the greatest emotional impact of Alaska, although others will doubtless disagree. This High Arctic area is a strange and haunting mixture of isolation, stillness, loneliness, and of grandeur and beauty too. It has an atmosphere born of the remoteness of vast spaces, alternately frightening and exhilarating. This is not an area that man should try and possess but rather one where he should

*Preceding pages* Storm clouds gather over the Chilkat River in south-east Alaska.

A wolf crosses the snow at the edge of the spruce forest. The wolf is one of the main natural predators of the barren-ground caribou.

walk with some degree of awe, a place of quiet and solitude where his intrusions should be kept to the minimum. It was in Arctic Alaska that I first realized that the appreciation of wilderness and wild nature is a creative act, to be likened to an appreciation of Beethoven's music or a Van Gogh painting.

Alaska stands now on the threshold of a new era, one which will undoubtedly bring more changes in a short space of time than have occurred in several preceding centuries. Mismanagement, greed, lack of imagination or a purely exploitive mentality on the part of those who will preside over these changes, could destroy for all time Alaska's unique wilderness and wildlife values. In their book *Wildlife in Alaska* published in 1953, Starker Leopold and Frank Fraser Darling (now Sir Frank Fraser Darling) wrote of how they were impressed with 'the grandeur and magnificence of this vast terrain' and wondered whether man with his modern technology 'was going to be the despoiler or the good steward of this last frontier'. It will not be long before we find out: the next ten to fifteen years will be the testing time.

I offer no apology for the 'purple prose' of this introduction to the book. I think it is indicative of the tremendous impact that Alaska has on most of those who, visiting her, get away from the cities. In the following chapters I shall be discussing some aspects of the fauna, flora and scenery of the various regions of Alaska, with particular emphasis on the Arctic. My aim is to be scientifically accurate and at the same time to convey as best I can something of the feeling and atmosphere of the wilderness.

In order to avoid any ambiguity, the scientific name of each animal and plant is given the first time the species is mentioned in the text, and the species are indexed under both common and scientific names. All scientific plant names are those used in the *Flora of Alaska and Neighboring Territories* by Eric Hultén, published by the Stanford University Press, California, in 1968. Where a species has an American and a British common name the American one is given first.

# Introducing Alaska

*There's a land where the mountains are nameless,*
*And the rivers all run God knows where;*
*There are lives that are erring and aimless,*
*And deaths that just hang by a hair;*
*There are hardships that nobody reckons;*
*There are valleys unpeopled and still;*
*There's a land—oh, it beckons and beckons,*
*And I want to go back—and I will.*

Robert Service

I have described the purpose of this book and my reasons for writing it, but even a book on wilderness and wildlife becomes more interesting if read with some knowledge of the history and general physical characteristics of the area concerned. To present such a background picture of Alaska is the purpose of this chapter.

Alaska today is a strange mixture of influences – Eskimo, Indian, Russian, American and, to a lesser extent, English. The English first set foot in Alaska long ago, but their participation in the oil discoveries represents the biggest stake they have had in Alaska's history to date. Perhaps the most famous Englishman to have come to Alaska was Captain James Cook who, in his search for the famed Northwest Passage, got as far north as Icy Cape, some 200 miles short of Barrow, in 1778. Other English explorers followed in his footsteps as a glance at the place names on the map of Arctic Alaska shows very well. In 1826 Captain John Franklin and Captain Frederick W. Beechey, approaching from the east and west respectively, endeavoured to link up on the north coast. It was the former who, for reasons that remain obscure, named the now famous Prudhoe Bay.

Appropriately enough in view of Alaska's mixed ethnic history, it was a Dane, Vitus Bering, sailing in the service of Tsar Peter the Great who discovered Alaska in 1741. He claimed it for Russia and died returning from it. The name Alaska is derived from an Aleut word variously rendered as Alaksu, Alakshak or Alashka, meaning Great Land. In the eighteenth century it was customary to work on the principle that a country was not 'discovered' until the white man had trodden its soil. In point of fact Alaska had been inhabited by Eskimos and Indians for many centuries before Vitus Bering sailed out of the mists to make his landfall in the south. His first view of the mainland of what was later to be called Alaska was the awe-inspiring snowy magnificence of Mount St Elias, 18,008 feet in height. By this time several quite distinct cultures had been developed by the natives, namely Aleuts, Eskimos, three Indian groups in the coastal regions of the south-east, and the more northerly Athapaskans. The ancestors of these Eskimos and Indians, like much of Alaska's fauna and flora, originally came from Siberia across the Bering Land Bridge, a connection that was formed and broken on several occasions from the Tertiary period to the Quaternary period. It would seem that the Bering Land Bridge saw two waves of human migration and there is evidence to suggest that the ancestors of the modern American Indian were the first to reach Alaska, possibly as early as 25,000 years ago.

Soon after Bering's discovery Russian America came into being, and Russian rule endured for 126 years. The Russians, however, saw very little of this vast country: the fifty or so communities that they established were all in the south and amounted to little more than tenuous toeholds on the perimeter of a great wilderness. By 1841 the profits from furs had dropped disastrously and Tsar Alexander II needed money to finance his war against the British in the Crimea. In addition the problems of governing a country so far removed from St Petersburg were immense and there were many who thought that this far flung colony could become a burden. After long and secret negotiations the Russians finally sold Alaska to the Americans in 1867 for the sum of 7.2 million dollars. Today this seems a laughable sum, particularly when viewed in the light of the 900 million dollar bid by the oil industry in September 1969 for 179 concession plots on the Arctic Slope.

The Russians interest in their new found territory was purely exploitive (an attitude that is still prevalent in certain quarters today) and they made tremendous inroads on the populations of the fur-

*Preceding pages* In Southern Alaska, fresh October snow cloaks the peaks of the Chugach Mountains and the spruce trees in Turnagain Pass.

bearing mammals and whales. A typical example was that of the sea otter(*Enhydra lutris*), an animal brought to the verge of extinction through being slaughtered for its beautiful fur. During a period of fifty-six years of Russian activity the *recorded* shipments of sea otter skins totalled over 186,000. A second exploitive phase in Alaska's history occurred in the late nineteenth century with the discovery of gold in the Klondike, and at Nome on the west coast at the turn of the century. In 1897 two tons of gold were brought out of Alaska on a single ship. Although the Klondike is in Canada the prospectors got to it through Alaska. The great gold bonanza lasted but a few years, and by 1907 Alaska had returned to oblivion.

Far removed from Washington, the Great Land slept more or less quietly for close on twenty years until, in 1923, the first major railroad link into the interior was completed and the pulse of commerce awakened. It was not, however, until June 1942, when Japanese bombers struck at the naval base of Dutch Harbour in the Aleutians and shortly thereafter their troops occupied the islands of Attu and Kiska, that Alaska sprung again into prominence. It has remained there ever since. Despite its enormous strategic importance, rich natural resources and other factors, it was not until January 1959 that Alaska was finally proclaimed the forty-ninth state of the United States of America and thus ceased to be merely a Territory. Two years earlier, in 1957, an important oil discovery was made on the Kenai Peninsula, on the east side of Cook Inlet to the south of Anchorage. Thus began another and perhaps the most significant phase in Alaska's history. The conservation problems resulting from the recent oil finds are briefly described in the next chapter.

Alaska has been a restless country whose progress has been spasmodic. Moving around the state the traveller finds abundant evidence of these earlier periods of brief glory. In the south-east are the onion-domed churches and place names such as Baranof and Petersburg that perpetuate the one and a quarter centuries of Russian rule. In the south-west, out on the barren and windswept Aleutian Islands, the battlefield relics are a rusting monument to the short-lived period of Japanese occupation. In central and western Alaska are some 300 ghost mines and ghost towns that recall the wild days of gold fever. In the High Arctic, an area where signs of the activities of early man are hardly noticeable, there are quite unmistakable signs of the presence of modern man – the white golf-ball domes of the early warning stations and the stark outlines of drilling rigs. So much for history, let us look now at the broad physical characteristics of the Great Land.

The outstanding features of Alaska are, of course, its sheer size and remoteness. With an area of 586,400 square miles or 375 million acres, it is about the size of Finland, Norway and Sweden combined; a little over six times the size of the United Kingdom; one-fifth the size of the United States and the largest of the states. The population of this vast area has only recently crept above the 300,000 level. This means that there are about 0.51 people per square mile as compared with about 594 per square mile in the United Kingdom. There is a great deal of elbow room in Alaska, particularly when it is realized that the bulk of the small population is concentrated in a few main centres such as Anchorage (accounting for almost half the population), Fairbanks and Juneau. It is interesting to note that almost the entire population lives below the 1000 foot contour. Extending as it does over some fifty-eight degrees of longitude from Hyder in south-east Alaska to Attu Island at the western tip of the Aleutian Islands, Alaska is remote from the rest of the United States (the 'lower forty-eight' to use an Alaskan phrase), but it is less than sixty miles from the Seward Peninsula across the Bering

*Above* High summer along the Chilkat River, near Haines in south-east Alaska, with the mountains reflected in the still waters.

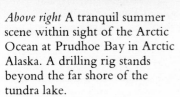
*Above right* A tranquil summer scene within sight of the Arctic Ocean at Prudhoe Bay in Arctic Alaska. A drilling rig stands beyond the far shore of the tundra lake.

*Right* The first snow of winter carpets a forest trail on the slopes of the Chugach Mountains in southern Alaska.

Sea to Siberia. The country also extends over four time zones and a resident of Ketchikan in the south-east is having lunch while his counterpart at Nome, situated on the Seward Peninsula, is just finishing breakfast.

Three climatic zones – arctic, subarctic and temperate – are represented in Alaska, and one third of this vast state lies to the north of the Arctic Circle. Alaska is predominantly a polar and sub-polar country. The mountainous relief of the country (sixty per cent of Alaska lies above the 3,300 foot contour) is the major factor responsible for these conditions. The high mountains in the south, notably the Alaska Range, successfully preclude penetration to the interior of warm air from the Pacific and the Gulf of Alaska, while somewhat lower mountains in the north and west permit the incursion of polar conditions to a large part of the country.

One of the most important physical factors in Alaska is permafrost which, in one form or another, underlies eighty-five per cent of the country. In the Arctic, permafrost is continuous, but becomes discontinuous and then sporadic as one moves southwards. Basically the only parts of Alaska without permafrost are the Aleutian Islands, Kenai Peninsula and The Panhandle. Permafrost may be defined as material, such as silt, sand, gravel or rock, the temperature of which has been below freezing point for two years or more. There are various categories of permafrost, but broadly speaking there are two main types. Dry permafrost contains little or no ice and typical examples of this type of permafrost are some of the gravel bars and terraces of the Arctic river valleys. Wet permafrost, on the other hand, has a high ice content and its presence is usually indicated by characteristic surface features. The most obvious of these features is the curious polygonal or patterned ground to be seen in its best form on the Arctic Slope. Permafrost exerts a profound influence on life in the north, affecting such things as vegetation, water supply, sewage disposal and construction. On the Arctic Slope oil drilling has shown that the permafrost extends downwards for at least 2,000 feet.

Almost everything in Alaska, like the state itself, is on the grand scale. It possesses some two-thirds of the United States' total continental shelf area, and it has nearly 35,000 miles of varied tidal shoreline. In the north are the shallow waters of the Arctic Ocean where coastal erosion may be as much as thirty feet per year; on the west coast are rugged cliffs and large delta areas, such as those of the Yukon and Kuskokwim Rivers which together cover 26,600 square miles; and travelling eastwards from the Aleutian Islands round the Gulf of Alaska one comes to the island-studded waters of The Panhandle in the extreme south-east. Here, in the magnificent fiord scenery of the Alexander Archipelago, there are said to be about 11,000 islands. The southern coastal area lies in the Circumpacific Earthquake Belt and is famous for its breathtaking scenery, its earthquakes and, in the Aleutian Islands, its volcanic activity.

When it comes to fresh water, Alaska is equally well endowed. The largest river system is of course that of the Yukon, which flows for 1,200 miles across central Alaska from the Canadian border in the east to the Bering Sea in the west, where it shares a vast delta complex with the Kuskokwim River. The catchment area of the Yukon River within Alaska is no less than 220,000 square miles. Other major rivers include the Copper, Susitna, Noatak and Colville, the last two being north of the Arctic Circle. There are reputed to be some three million lakes of twenty acres or more in size, ninety-four of which have an area of ten square miles or more. The largest lakes are in the south-west and are Lake Iliamna (1,000 square miles) and Lake Becharof (458 square miles).

These rank second and fifth in size for lakes within the entire United States. On the Arctic Slope the largest body of fresh water is Lake Teshekpuk which covers some 315 square miles. With all this wealth of wetland habitat it is hardly surprising that about a third of all North America's waterfowl come to Alaska to breed in summer.

Although a considerable proportion of Alaska lies beyond the northern limit of tree growth, the state contains sixteen per cent of all forest land within the United States, that is to say about 186,000 square miles of which approximately 44,000 square miles are classed as commercial. There is as much forest in Alaska as in the states of California, Montana, Oregon and Washington combined, but the average quality is much lower. It is in the coastal areas of the south that the finest and best developed forests are to be found, that is to say round the Gulf of Alaska and in particular in the humid high rainfall area of The Panhandle. The bulk of these forests are within the 8,000 square mile Chugach National Forest and the 25,000 square mile Tongass National Forest, the latter being the largest national forest in the United States. These fine coastal forests are a northern extension of the rainforests of the Cascades and coastal ranges of Washington, Oregon and British Columbia. They are dominated by Sitka spruce (*Picea sitchensis*), and western hemlock (*Tsuga heterophylla*) which accounts for ninety-six per cent of the coastal forests, with the occasional mountain hemlock, (*T. mertensiana*) and Alaska cedar (*Chamaecyparis nootkatensis*). It may be noted that Alaska has about eighty-eight per cent of all Sitka spruce in the United States. The topography of the south-east coastal region is rugged with slopes rising 2,000 to 3,000 feet within three miles or less of the tideline.

The second main area of forest lies in the Alaskan interior, an area of varied topography and climate where permafrost, low precipitation, high water tables, thin soils and frequent forest fires combine to make tree growth relatively sparse over wide areas. The main forested areas of this part of the state lie in the drainages of the Susitna, Copper, Tanana, Yukon and Kuskokwim Rivers and consist of a mixture of white spruce (*Picea glauca*), black spruce (*P. mariana*), paper birch (*Betula papyrifera*), quaking aspen (*Populus tremuloides*), and balsam poplar (*P. balsamifera*). Within these interior forests the white spruce is the predominant species, particularly on well drained soils. The black spruce is pretty well confined to the extensive stretches of boggy lowlands, the 'muskeg' of the Algonquin Indians. These boreal forests die out on the southern slopes of the Brooks Range.

Mention was made earlier of the mountainous and rugged nature of Alaska, a point underlined by the fact that the fourteen highest mountain peaks in the United States lie within the state, and Mount McKinley at 20,320 feet is the highest mountain in North America. A glance at the topographical map shows that for broad descriptive purposes Alaska is conveniently divided into several major sections by mountain ranges. From north to south these divisions are the Arctic Slope, the Brooks Range, the intermontane plateaus of interior Alaska, the southern mountain arcs comprising the Alaska and Aleutian Ranges and associated groups, and the Gulf of Alaska area. These divisions are mostly continuations of features found in the western United States and Canada.

Standing at the edge of the Arctic Ocean on a crystal clear day and looking southwards one can see the Brooks Range. These mountains are an extension of the Rocky Mountain system which bends westwards as it reaches the Alaskan–Canadian border in the vicinity of the Arctic Ocean. It forms a rugged barrier extending westwards across Alaska for about 600 miles to the sea. In the east the peaks rise to a little over 9,000 feet, but they are lower and gentler in the west. The Brooks Range actually consists of a number of individual mountain groups bearing the names of their explorers or discoverers. In the east are the Romanzof and Davidson Mountains; the Franklin and Sadlerochit Mountains are in the Canning River drainage system; the Philip Smith Mountains span the headwaters of the Canning and Sagavanirktok Rivers where the valley of the latter forms part of the route of the trans-Alaska crude oil pipeline; the Endicott Mountains are in the centre of the range; and the western end is formed by the DeLong, Baird and Schwatka Mountains. The highest peaks in the range are found in the Canning River area. They are the 9,020 foot Mount Chamberlain in the Franklin Mountains and the 8,855 foot Mount Michelson in the Romanzof Mountains, but Mount Doonerak in the Endicott Mountains is 8,500 feet high.

The Brooks Range acquired its present form in the late Tertiary period, ten to twenty million years ago, and subsequent uplift, erosion and glaciation all played a part in sculpturing the mountains to their existing appearance. Many small cliff and valley glaciers and U-shaped valleys provide evidence of earlier glacial activity. The Endicott and Romanzof Mountains have a very marked saw-toothed outline. There are few low passes through the Brooks Range, the best and most widely used being Anaktuvuk Pass at 2,200 feet between the northerly

*Below* In the beautiful Matanuska Valley, in the Chugach Mountains, fall colours frame the distant Matanuska Glacier.

*Right* Storms and snow herald the onset of winter in the forests of the Chugach Mountains.

*Below right* Clouds swirl around the summit of Mount McKinley in the Alaska Range. At 20,320 feet, this is the highest mountain in North America.

flowing Anaktuvuk River and the southward flowing John River. In this pass is the only inland Eskimo settlement in Alaska.

In describing southern Alaska it is difficult to avoid using too many superlatives. The breathtaking beauty of the fiord and forest scenery has already been touched upon. These southern mountains are quite different in character from the Brooks Range, and as the Pacific mountain system they are a continuation of the coastal mountain system of the western United States and Canada. Basically there are two arcs of mountains, the northernmost and largest of which comprises the Coast Mountains in the south-east where they straddle the Alaskan–Canadian border, the Alaska Range together with the Aleutian Range and Islands which it joins in the west, and the Wrangell Mountains with which it connects in the east. The smaller southern arc consists of the island mountains of The Panhandle, the Fairweather Range, the St Elias Mountains, the Chugach Mountains, and the mountains of Kenai

Peninsula and Kodiak Island. A study of the map shows that the two arcs are separated by a trough consisting of the Inside Passage in The Panhandle, the Copper River lowlands, Cook Inlet and the Susitna River lowlands, and Shelikof Strait which separates Kodiak Island from the Aleutians. The Wrangell and Talkeetna Mountains intrude into this trough. The Gulf of Alaska area is a predominantly mountainous arcuate belt 800 miles long and from 20 to 110 miles wide, extending from Kodiak Island in the west to Cross Sound in the east.

That extreme south-east part of Alaska known as The Panhandle is a narrow, rugged strip of country hugging the edge of British Columbia, and its mountains drop steeply into the sea. This 'handle' is connected to the 'pan' by the St Elias Mountains, which are the highest coastal mountains in the world and lie partly in Canada. They form a vast, desolate, ice-bound region apparently limitless in expanse, with hundreds of angular mountain peaks. These peaks include the 19,850 foot Mount Logan and the 18,008 foot Mount St Elias, which rank as the second and fourth highest peaks on the North American continent, as well as a dozen others that exceed in altitude the highest in the continental United States.

The St Elias Mountains are topographically continuous with and geologically similar to the Chugach Mountains. The Chugach and Kenai Mountains comprise the 450 mile long central section of mountains bordering the Gulf of Alaska, and vary in width from 30 to 110 miles. They are extremely rugged with the average relief of their valley walls being at least 5,000 feet. There are a number of high peaks in the Chugach Mountains and the southern front overlooking the coastal lowlands east of the Copper River delta includes Mount Miller at 11,000 feet and Mount Steller at 12,023 feet. The Kenai Mountains are simply an extension of the Chugach Mountains from which they are separated by Turnagain Arm. Their highest peak at 6,800 feet is still unnamed. The cluster of mountainous islands of which Kodiak Island is the largest, are again a continuation of the Chugach and Kenai Mountains.

Driving southwards from Glennallen along the Richardson Highway towards Valdez one can see the Wrangell Mountains to the east. Rising to an altitude of more than 10,000 feet above the Copper River plateau, they are beautiful indeed with more than a dozen peaks soaring to over 12,000 feet above sea level. The Wrangells are a compact cluster of volcanic mountains lying between the Alaska Range to the north and the Chugach Mountains to the south. Mount Wrangell itself rises to an altitude of 14,163 feet, but is exceeded by Mount Blackburn at 16,523 feet, and Mount Sanford at 16,208 feet. The eruptions that produced the Wrangell Mountains began in the early Tertiary, perhaps around fifty million years ago, and have continued spasmodically ever since.

Rugged and heavily glaciated throughout its 600 mile length, the Alaska Range is a huge arcuate mountain wall merging gradually with the Aleutian Range in the west, and separated by narrow passes from the Wrangell Mountains in the east. Oddly enough, although the highest mountain in North America (Mount McKinley at 20,320 feet) is in this range, it contains few other really high mountains, with less than twenty peaks exceeding 10,000 feet in height. Mount McKinley is particularly impressive as it rises from a base plain only 3,000 feet above sea level: its steep north face for instance is 15,000 feet high. Its close neighbour, Mount Foraker is almost as impressive, being 17,395 feet high. Further east and lying north of the Denali Highway is another quite massive group in the Alaska Range, dominated by Mount Hayes, at 13,700 feet, and Mount Deborah, at 12,540 feet. Even at the height of summer the Alaska Range presents from the air an awesome scene of jagged snow-covered peaks and icefields.

At the centre of present volcanic activity in Alaska are the Aleutian Islands and the Alaska Peninsula, whose peaks rise to an average height of 9,000 feet, most of them being volcanoes. The Aleutian Range stretches for 1,600 miles from the 11,070 foot Mount Spurr, opposite Anchorage, to the island of Attu at the tip of the chain, and within this distance some eighty volcanoes have been identified. There is continuing crustal activity in the Aleutians and Mount Shishaldin, 9,978 feet high, is known as 'Smoking Moses' among sailors because of its glow at night. Rugged, bleak, barren and storm-swept, the Aleutians to many will be the least attractive part of Alaska.

At the head of the Aleutians lies the 4,200 square miles of rugged country comprising Katmai National Monument. It was here in June 1912 that the most spectacular Alaskan eruption in historic time occurred, when Novarupta Volcano blew with a thunderous blast. Shortly afterwards the summit of nearby Mount Katmai collapsed inwards to form a caldera approximately three miles by two miles in extent. More than seven cubic miles of pumice and broken rock were hurled into the sky during these eruptions, and some forty square miles of the valley floor was buried to depths of up to 700 feet. This subsequently became known as the Valley of 10,000 Smokes, but all but one or two of the formerly numerous fumaroles have long been inactive.

Before concluding this brief account of the history and more outstanding physical features of Alaska, mention must be made of glaciers and icefields, of which there are about 51,000 square miles within the state, that is to say they cover about 8.7 per cent of the total area of Alaska. The Brooks Range in the north has, as stated earlier, only small cliff and valley glaciers and a few ice fields, but in southern Alaska it is a different story. In fact the most striking scenic features of south-east Alaska are due to massive glaciation, a result of heavy precipitation and high elevations. The Chugach, Kenai and St Elias Mountains contain the most extensive system of valley glaciers and some of the largest ice fields in North America. Glaciation is also a widespread phenomenon in the Alaska Range and great glaciers radiate from Mount McKinley and other peaks. The Mount McKinley complex has in fact a continuous network of large valley glaciers, such as the Muldrow, Eldridge and Kahiltna Glaciers.

It is, however, to south-east Alaska that one goes to see the ultimate in Alaskan glacial scenery, for here on the coastal side of the mountains most glaciers descend below 500 feet and many reach tidewater. Superb glacial scenery may be seen in the Glacier Bay National Monument (the largest in the National Parks system) to the north-west of Juneau. Glaciers that debouch from narrow valleys on to coastal plains and spread out to form a lobe or fan are known as piedmont glaciers and one of the largest in North America is of this type. This is the 810 square mile Malaspina Glacier, with its forty mile wide front, near Yakutat. Near its centre the ice is about 2,000 feet thick. The Bering Glacier further up the coast is almost as large. In the western Chugach Mountains the huge ice fields around Mount Witherspoon give birth to the Columbia Glacier which runs for over forty miles down to the sea in Prince William Sound. One can reach this glacier by boat from Valdez and get close in to the face, an awesome mass of steely-blue ice three miles wide, towering from 300 to 500 feet above the water and reaching 200 feet below the surface to bedrock.

In the following chapters we shall be taking a further look at the various regions of Alaska and their scenery, with particular reference to the fauna and flora associated with them.

# Conservation
# and Development

*'In wildness is the preservation of the world.'*
Henry David Thoreau

IT is possible that by the time that this book is published construction will have started on the trans-Alaska crude oil pipeline from Prudhoe Bay in the north to the ice-free port of Valdez on the Gulf of Alaska in the south, a distance of nearly 800 miles. If such proves to be the case, then it means that what has been described by one American writer as 'the most monumental confrontation ever between industry and the conservation movement' will have entered its final phase. Opposition to oil industry plans to move oil from the Arctic Slope culminated, in April 1970, in the conservation movement filing suit in Washington D.C. This action resulted in a preliminary injunction restraining the Secretary of the Interior from issuing permits which would allow pipeline construction to begin. This injunction was lifted in the fall of 1972.

Many people have little idea of the costs involved in a major industrial project such as the proposed trans-Alaska pipeline. The original estimate of the cost of the project in 1969 was 900 million dollars, and by 1972 this had risen to around 3,000 million dollars. Much of this increase is due to improved design criteria and other factors, and some is a direct result of the delay imposed by the legal action. It is not possible to assess the respective proportions.

It is not the purpose of this chapter to discuss the rights or wrongs of the pipeline, about which a voluminous literature already exists and more will doubtless be added. What I wish to do is look at the general philosophy of the problem of development in relation to conservation in Alaska and to present some of the widely differing points of view. There is no point in bemoaning the fact that large reserves of oil have been discovered in Arctic Alaska, because it is a fact of life that they have. The crucial requirement now is to develop them without impairing the unique quality of the Alaskan environment, and this depends on various factors, many of which are beyond the control of the oil industry. In my opinion oil has, unfortunately, been only the catalyst in the current furore on the subject of development in Alaska. It is an argument that was bound to come sooner or later for one reason or another.

In considering conservation and development in Alaska it is first of all necessary to sketch in some historical background. For many years after the Russians came upon Alaska in 1741 and established Russian America, the economy of the country went in fits and starts with long periods of quiescence between booms. First there was the gross exploitation of fur-bearing mammals, particularly of marine mammals, by the Russians. By 1841 revenue from this source had sunk to a low level, and this was doubtless one of the factors in Russia's decision to sell Alaska to the United States.

Having acquired Alaska, the United States government virtually ignored it until 1884 when it was assigned a governor appointed by Washington. In the late nineteenth and early twentieth centuries came the gold rush, a period of boom and profit. By 1907 the tide turned and it was all over – Alaska returned to oblivion.

In the 1940s Alaska's strategic position precipitated the defence rush which brought a lot of money and people into the country. Other than the fairly steady contribution to the economy provided by military spending since the Second World War, Alaska's main source of income has been from the harvesting of renewable, natural resources such as fish and lumber – a fragile and seasonal economy narrowly based. Then in 1957 came the first important oil discovery on the Kenai Peninsula and with it the birth of disagreement between the conservationists and the oil industry in Alaska.

The emergence of Alaska as the forty-ninth state of the Union took

*Preceding pages* At 2 am on a June night, a shaft of sunlight strikes through a gap in the black storm clouds to illuminate the ice on Galbraith Lake in the northern foothills of the Brooks Range.

seventy-five years to come about from the time the first governor was appointed by Washington in 1884. The proclamation of statehood was signed by President Dwight Eisenhower on 3rd January 1959. This act gave Alaska the right to select and take title from the Federal Government of some 103 million acres from the total of 375 million acres within the state boundaries; this selection is still uncompleted at the time of writing.

Alaska's greatest need on achieving statehood was to achieve a firm economic base that would give freedom from reliance on federal aid. This was only fractionally realized by the three major wells that were producing on the Kenai Peninsula by 1959 and, in the early 1960s, by over a dozen offshore wells in Cook Inlet. The discovery, in 1968 and 1969 by Atlantic Richfield, Humble Oil and British Petroleum, of the biggest oil reserves in North America, beneath the Arctic Slope, changed the whole picture. Here, at last, was a non-renewable resource that promised huge cash returns and a relatively stable economy, and the 'black gold rush' became a fact.

However, along with the discovery of oil in the Arctic came something else too, the environmental revolution. Steadily gathering a momentum that is now worldwide, was the thought that the quality of life depended upon the maintenance of unspoilt areas of wilderness where man could find aesthetic and spiritual inspiration.

In Alaska it was upon the oil industry that the wrath of the conservationists descended. The oil industry, however, has not by any means been the only one to come into conflict with the environmentalists. The United States Forest Service, for example, has been severely criticized over its logging policies in the Tongass National Forest, and the Atomic Energy Commission had a tough fight over their underground nuclear explosions in the Aleutians. Earlier still, the United States Army Corps of Engineers stirred up a hornet's nest with their proposal to dam the Yukon River at Rampart. I like to think that the response of the major oil companies to genuine fears of the conservationists has been a reasonable one.

It has frequently been said that many Alaskans are sick to death of being told by 'outsiders' what they should or should not do in Alaska as regards industrial and related developments. No doubt it is true that the majority of Alaskans are in favour of the pipeline for economic reasons. Given wisdom and planning the state should, with its oil-derived revenues, be able to improve greatly the lot of the average Alaskan through a variety of much-needed social investment projects.

The question of who owns Alaska depends to some extent on one's point of view. In terms of hard figures over two-thirds of Alaska is federal territory. The views of the Eskimos and Indians were made clear by the Alaska native land claims which were only settled by an Act of Congress in December 1971 which allows the natives to take title to forty million acres throughout the state. Without losing sight of the fact that the interests of the citizens of Alaska must be a prime consideration, it can be argued on a philosophical basis that the abundant wildlife and superb wilderness of Alaska belong not only to all Americans, but should be regarded as being held in trust as an international treasure for the enjoyment of future generations. I hope that those who read this book will decide for themselves what the Alaska of the future should be like, and I hope that what I have written and portrayed will convince them that Alaska's scenery and wildlife form a combination that cannot be found elsewhere.

To simplify matters, I suppose one can recognize three categories into which opinions on the subject of conservation and development in Alaska can be placed. At one extreme are those who are reaching for an

*Above* In the spruce forest of southern Alaska, a large brown bear is sleepy after a heavy meal of salmon, caught in the Brooks River.

*Below* For many decades barren-ground caribou have migrated across the coastal tundra at Prudhoe Bay. The presence of drilling rigs has not so far caused them to change this long-established habit.

unattainable utopia and say that all of Alaska's remaining wilderness should remain so. At the opposite extreme stand those who are motivated solely by economic and short-term gains, and who would like to be given carte blanche to develop what they like, where they like and how they like. Alaska has suffered too much from this type in the past. In the centre are those who believe that it is possible to achieve a satisfactory balance between these opposing views, given the right approach by those in power. The whole issue is charged with a great deal of emotion.

Now there is no doubt that there do exist in Alaska powerful groups with an interest in increasing growth and opening up the country

*Right* Mid-winter in the Gulkana Basin, where bright moonlight reveals the weird shapes of snow-covered spruce trees.

for development. All over the state there are monuments to past ephemeral exploitation and unplanned development, but the sheer size of Alaska has dissipated their effects. With the technology now available and the type of developments likely in the future, this would not be the case. A classic example is the winter haul road from Fairbanks to Prudhoe Bay. Bulldozed out during the winter of 1968 to 1969, it has been described by an American writer as 'one of the most disgraceful environmental and financial disasters that have occurred in Alaska; a watery monument to politics, expediency and a frontier frenzy to open up the country'. This road has been completely impassable ever since the winter of 1969 to 1970.

There can be few so insensitive as to suggest that the wilderness and wildlife resources of Alaska, together with the intangible spiritual benefits that go with them, are unimportant and can simply be written off. It is these very things that underpin the tourist industry. Under careful management these renewable resources should continue in perpetuity.

Oil, on the other hand, is a finite resource, but as the full extent of Alaska's reserves is still unknown it is not possible to say how long they will last. But we can say that, if things are done properly, people will still be coming to Alaska to see the largest gathering of brown bears in the world long after the oil has gone.

Let us take the middle course and accept the fact that economics, politics and the present way of life, with its enormous dependence on petroleum products, dictate that Alaskan oil must be utilized. Let us also agree that it is possible to do this and at the same time to preserve the wilderness and wildlife values. Why is it that many of the realistic conservationists who do accept these facts are still very uneasy about the future prospects?

Basically they are worried because so much recent development in Alaska has happened very quickly with, at least at the start, no effective control by the authorities. They are worried that ecologically bad projects, such as the winter haul road, might be repeated. They see new national park and wilderness area proposals bitterly opposed by would-be developers. They know that too many people pay little more than lip service to conservation. In brief they feel a lack of faith in the ability of those in power to control the situation.

Politically the situation in Alaska is rendered complicated to the English eye by the involvement of both Federal and State Governments. In March 1972 Secretary of the Interior Rogers C. B. Morton, in what he described as 'an historic moment', set aside 227 million acres of public lands in Alaska under the authority granted him by the Alaska Native Claims Settlement Act of 1972. These with-drawals include eighty million acres for possible inclusion in the national park, wildlife refuge, wild and scenic rivers, and forest systems; 1.8 million acres for replacement of wildlife refuges which might be selected by Alaska natives; and 1.2 million acres for a gas and oil pipeline corridor.

The state administration, more concerned with economic develop-ment, disagrees with some of these withdrawals. Two weeks after the Secretary of the Interior's action, the state continued to threaten filing suit against the Department of the Interior in an attempt to secure some of these areas for state ownership.

Clearly there will be pressures and problems in the future. The tapping of the Prudhoe Bay oil reserves as at present planned will provide an access route to parts of northern Alaska never before accessible by road. Public access from these new roads into adjacent wilderness areas could have a disastrous effect on the wildlife, unless controls are established to limit the use of, for example, all-terrain vehicles and snowmobiles. Similar situations could arise with access routes elsewhere in Alaska where there are large potential oil reserves, as for example under the Chukchi Sea or in the Gulf of Alaska area. Alaska is also full of other minerals that have not been fully exploited – coal, copper, tin, platinum and iron to mention but a few. With the changing economic picture and increased access to remote areas, there are bound to be moves to tap these resources.

With a steadily increasing annual revenue the State Government will have the financial means to embark upon many diverse schemes that were not possible before. Obviously many potentially serious problems will arise, most of them totally unrelated to the question of oil, and others only indirectly connected.

Without a doubt there is a challenge. Despite all that has happened in the past there is still a chance and just enough time to achieve the right balance. To do so will require imagination, great foresight, bravery and a revolution in attitudes on the part of all concerned, but particularly at government level. Development at any cost is a philosophy that is no longer acceptable. Yet it still exists. What Alaska cannot afford is to be guided by sentiments such as those expressed by a former state official who in 1970 said 'Hell, this country's so goddam big that even if industry ran wild we could never wreck it. We can have our cake and eat it too'. Experience elsewhere has shown that the cake soon vanishes.

There is a need for the greatest and most imaginative land-use plan ever conceived anywhere in the world. Alaska has all that demands and deserves this.

More wilderness areas and national parks must be created. Communication routes, development areas and centres of population must be planned on a very long term basis, with a view to causing minimum disruption to the wilderness. Perhaps there should even be a limit to the maximum population in Alaska. All developments that take place in Alaska should occur, not in isolation, but as part of an overall national planning policy, a policy that would make due allowance for all interests and ensure a decent heritage for future generations. While the land freeze was in force no such planning was possible, but there is now evidence of a movement in this direction.

Alaska has it within her grasp to do what no other country has really achieved, to develop her economy and at the same time preserve in perpetuity perhaps the finest combination of wilderness scenery and wildlife in the world today. It was in the United States during Theodore Roosevelt's presidency, that the idea of conservation in the form that we understand it today first took shape. What an unhappy twist of fate it would be if the same nation presided over the demise of The Last Great Wilderness.

What will the future Alaska be like? There are men in the state now with the imagination to see what it *could* be like. One of them is Dr Robert Weeden who has disagreed with some of the things I have written in the past, but I wish to conclude this chapter with his vision of the future Alaska:–

'The future Alaska I rather wistfully envision would have more people than now – perhaps 500,000 or so – but they would be in the same population centers as now. There would be awesome stretches of semi-wilderness where people lived who prized solitude or who enjoyed making their way from the seasonal fruits of the countryside. There would be relatively smaller stretches of true wilderness, balanced by local areas where facilities were developed for the enjoyment of nature by larger numbers of visitors. There would be a comfortable network of roads where needed, planned, mile by mile, to display and preserve the countryside and to host appropriate commercial, residential and recreational uses. Public revenues would come from the usual range of personal and corporate taxes and from the State's share of Alaskan resources extracted for private profit: oil, gas, fish, minerals, timber, water.

'In a very real sense what I am proposing is not only a milieu for Alaskans but an opportunity for the world. The world needs an embodiment of the frontier mythology, the sense of horizons unexplored, the mystery of uninhabited miles. It needs a place where wolves stalk the strand lines in the dark, because a land that can produce a wolf is a healthy, robust and perfect land.'

# The Arctic Slope
# and the Brooks Range

*Have you ever heard of the Land of Beyond,*
*That dreams at the gates of the day?*
*Alluring it lies at the skirts of the skies,*
*And ever so far away;*
*Alluring it calls: O ye the yoke galls,*
*And ye of the trail overfond,*
*With saddle and pack, by paddle and track,*
*Let's go to the Land of Beyond.*

Robert Service

**W**HAT is the Arctic? On studying this question we find that it is a term that is not at all easy to define. To administrators and attorneys it is anywhere north of the Arctic Circle at latitude 66°33′N, but this definition has no biological significance. The Arctic is in fact an imprecisely defined area embracing the polar seas and the bare and desolate tundra lands that surround them. Biologically speaking, the logical southern limit of the Arctic coincides with the beginning of boreal coniferous forest. This is a very convenient boundary which, in point of fact, approximates very closely to the 50°F July isotherm. Wladamir Köppen devised a system of climatic classification in which he defined a polar climate as one in which the mean temperature of the warmest month does not exceed 50°F. A glance at a map on which the northern limit of forest growth and the 50°F July isotherm are indicated shows how closely they coincide.

The Arctic (North) Slope of Alaska is the High Arctic so far as Alaska is concerned, but internationally speaking it is not really the High Arctic at all, since the North Pole lies well over 1,000 miles further north. Nevertheless, to plants and animals it is a harsh environment and the variety of species found there is much less than is the case further south in temperate and tropical areas, although the actual numbers of some individual species may be very high. One of the fascinating aspects of the Arctic ecosystem is its relative biological simplicity.

To most people the term 'Arctic' is synonymous with biting cold, but this is only partly true. Those who have travelled the northlands know the Arctic in many moods. Vilhalmur Stefansson, one of the last dog team explorers of Arctic Alaska, called a book that he wrote in 1921 *The Friendly Arctic*. Certainly it is hostile at times and during the sixty-five dark, sunless days of winter one tends to wonder why anyone would want to live or work in such a place. Take Prudhoe Bay for example on a cold and dark December day. The air temperature may only be −30°F, but a powerful wind off the polar ice introduces a chill factor which can bring the effective temperature three times lower than this, or more. If there is a 'white out' as there often is, then visibility may become a matter of a few feet. Under conditions such as these it requires a great deal of imagination to accept that in the past dense forest and grassland extended north to the shores of an ice-free Arctic Ocean, but such was the case.

One of the fascinating by-products of drilling in the search for oil is the evidence of conditions in past ages that is found in the cores brought to the surface. Among the evidence obtained during the course of drilling at Prudhoe Bay have been fossilized cones and other fossilized plant remains, including pollen grains, that make it possible to reconstruct past climates. Fossil material in cores from about 500 feet and 1,800 feet includes virtually complete cones of a species of spruce (almost certainly Sitka spruce) as well as pollen spores of pine and hemlock. These indicate the presence of rich boreal coniferous forest in the immediate vicinity of Prudhoe Bay at the time these remains were deposited, which is considered to have been in the early or mid-Miocene period, approximately fifteen million or twenty-five million years ago. At that time the mean July temperature at Prudhoe Bay must have been at least 53°F, that is to say it was rather warmer than at present.

Let us look a little more closely at this intriguing area, the Arctic Slope, as it is now. It is quite well defined with the Arctic Ocean to the north, the Bering Sea to the west, the Canadian border to the east, and the great wall of the Brooks Range to the south. Altogether it is an area

*Preceding pages* Clear waters, quiet valleys, and nameless snow-covered mountains are typical of the Brooks Range. This is June in the Atigun River valley, in the northern foothills.

*Opposite* An Arctic fox in the white coat of winter. In Arctic Alaska this fox ranges out on the polar pack ice, where it scavenges after the polar bear. On the tundra its diet includes Arctic ground squirrels and lemmings.

of some 56.6 million acres of tundra and mountain foothills. In the frigid grip of winter, when snow blankets the ground and it is difficult to say where the tundra ends and the sea begins, animal life is sparse and not very obvious. Nevertheless, life exists both above and below the snow. In the former case, with one or two exceptions such as the raven (*Corvus corax*), the birds and animals that are present are in their white winter plumage or pelage. This white winter coloration adopted by so many Arctic birds and animals serves two purposes. It provides good camouflage against the snow, and it allows solar radiation to penetrate and warm the body.

The Arctic fox (*Alopex lagopus*) is among the first animals that one is likely to notice in winter, and it has shown little difficulty in adapting to the presence of modern man on the Arctic Slope. At Prudhoe Bay

In summer, the Arctic fox moults into a piebald coat that is much thinner than the winter coat, and it dens in pingos and raised ridges on the tundra.

one of these foxes lived for a considerable time beneath a small shed strategically located close to the door of the cookhouse. For some peculiar reason they have developed a liking for seismic survey cables, so much so that there have been occasions when work has been held up for a long time because foxes had chewed through the cables almost as soon as they had been laid on the tundra. Away from the temptations of the artefacts provided by man, the Arctic fox is a true scavenger to whom very little comes amiss. Like various other Arctic animals the numbers of this fox fluctuate considerably and are closely related to the troughs and peaks of the markedly cyclic lemming populations. These and other small rodents, when present, are often active beneath the snow in winter and form an important item in the diet of the fox.

Two birds that come in for mention at this point are the snowy owl (*Nyctea scandiaca*) and the willow ptarmigan (*Lagopus lagopus*). The former, like the Arctic fox, is dependent for food on the small rodents but to a greater extent than the fox. Very low rodent populations mean very few magnificent snowy owls on the tundra. When the tundra is snow-covered, however, the snowy owl will frequently take willow ptarmigan and snow buntings (*Plectrophenax nivalis*), the latter being one of the few small passerine birds that one can expect to see on the tundra towards the end of winter, since it returns quite early. It is a joy to watch a snowy owl gliding low and silently across the white expanse of tundra in search of ptarmigan. It is indeed quite remarkable how they see the birds at all unless they move, for when motionless the willow ptarmigan in winter plumage is all but invisible against the snow. The willow ptarmigan is, however, an abundant bird, particularly in river valleys where low willow scrub is most common. I have seen flocks of up to 400 ptarmigan in the Echooka, Ivishak and Sagavanirktok River valleys in the fall, and in spring flocks numbering thousands have been seen. They flush abruptly and startlingly as one nears them, fly for a short distance and settle again on the snow.

It is not, however, the majestic snowy owl quartering the frozen tundra, nor the awe-inspiring expanse of frozen sea stretching north into the limitless distance that epitomizes the Arctic winter, but a phenomenon associated with the heavens. To those who live in Alaska, the Aurora Borealis, or Northern Lights, is a regular feature of winter and a never failing delight. For those who come from a part of the world where such a sight is unknown the Aurora Borealis is truly magnificent, a display once seen never forgotten. The winter skies in the Arctic are beautiful anyway, filled with sheets of stars on a background of the darkest blue-black. But when the dancing lights are added the scene becomes one that requires the skill of a good poet to adequately describe. My very first sight of the Aurora Borealis was in the third week of September 1969 when I was based at an airstrip known as Sagwon, which is in the Sagavanirktok Valley, some seventy miles south of the Arctic Ocean.

We had flown over a large area of country by helicopter during the day, studying the late fall movements of the barren-ground caribou (*Rangifer tarandus*) for a research project that lasted for six weeks or so. Sitting in a helicopter for hours can be tiring and later, after a good supper, I felt like stretching my legs in a walk under the stars. It was about two hours before midnight and, radiating from a single point, three long fingers of greenish light lanced across the sky. This was fascinating, but only a prelude of what was to come on subsequent occasions when the Aurora illumined the cold nights, shedding a ghostly glow on the tundra. How incredible are some of these displays when red, green and blue flames form curtains and roll up only to unfold again, or take the form of arcs and rays, but all the time dancing, shimmering and flickering. The physicist can tell us that this flickering light is produced by the excitation of atoms in a rarefied gas. But to see the Aurora Borealis in the Arctic night sky is an experience that cannot be properly described in the cold words of science.

The tundra is often said to be a cold desert, and certainly in terms of precipitation it can be placed in that category. There are some interesting similarities between night on the tundra and night in the Sahara Desert. Both can be cold and both have star-studded skies. Again, in both cases, there is a feeling of vast and uncluttered distance. This cold desert of Alaska has an annual precipitation of 50 to 250 millimetres per year. There are even similarities between the physiology of some of the mammals found in the Alaskan desert and those found in the Sahara. The water metabolism of the musk ox (*Ovibos moschatus*), for instance, is similar to that of the camel.

Even the long Arctic winter has an ending, although the snow and ice remain for some time after the days have brightened. But between the latter part of May and mid-June the slowly increasing warmth of the sun produces a steady if irregular thaw. Leads of open water appear on the lakes of the coastal tundra and the sky fills with flights of ducks, geese and waders; the Arctic Slope comes to life and the short Arctic summer is about to begin.

It is at this time that many things begin to happen fairly rapidly. As the tundra pools clear of ice the open areas of water are quickly occupied by hundreds of shorebirds. Paramount among these are the red or grey phalarope (*Phalaropus fulicarius*) and the northern or red-necked phalarope (*P. lobatus*) with the former predominating. Both species breed on the Arctic Slope, with the northern replacing the red as the most common species as one travels from the coast towards the mountains. The red phalarope assumes a distinctive breeding plumage of a deep brick-red, a condition in which it is not seen in the British Isles where it occurs only as a migrant or occasional winter visitor. However the northern phalarope does breed in the Scottish islands, where I have watched them pirouetting amongst the buckbean (*Meryanthes trifoliata*) growing in the small lakes. Other waders also appear by these tundra pools, feeding with an air of intensive urgency along the edge of the water. These include the dunlin (*Erolia alpina*), the stilt sandpiper (*Micropalama himantopus*), the semi-palmated sandpiper (*Ereunetes pusillus*) and the pectoral sandpiper (*Erolia melanotus*).

Ducks too appear in force, particularly the common eider (*Somateria mollissima*) and the king eider (*S. spectabilis*), but also the mallard (*Anas platyrhynchos*), shoveler (*Spatula clypeata*), American wigeon (*Mareca americana*), pintail (*Anas acuta*), green-winged teal (*A. carolinensis*), oldsquaw or long-tailed duck (*Clangula hyemalis*), greater scaup (*Aythya marila*), and the white-winged scoter (*Melanitta deglandi*). Grazing on the grass just appearing through the last thin layer of snow are the geese – Canada geese (*Branta canadensis*), black brants (*B. nigricans*), and white-fronted geese (*Anser albifrons*). Pairs of whistling swans (*Olor columbianus*) and loons appear on the water, and flying restlessly about is that most beautiful of the Arctic breeding gulls, Sabine's gull (*Xema sabini*).

Restlessness and excitement are the operative words at the very beginning of the Arctic summer in northern Alaska. This fever is evident on every hand. Along the coast there is a steady passage eastwards towards Canada of geese, ducks and shorebirds. Not hundreds but tens of hundreds of birds are involved, the total probably running well into seven figures. Is there any other sight which can set the blood tingling through one's veins in quite the same way as skein after skein of wild geese forging steadily across the blue Arctic sky, a sky that has been empty through the long dark days of winter? All geese are exciting in such a setting, but none more so than the snow geese (*Chen hyperborea*) whose pure white plumage is relieved only by the black wing tips. Frequently one can hear the calls of the geese long before they can be seen, because sound travels far in the crisp, cold conditions.

The air of urgency is very evident as one watches the phalaropes on open areas of water. I have seen up to 300 and more of these birds on one piece of water and at first sight it seems that they are engaged in a frenzy of pointless activity. Closer observation shows that this is not so. Most of them are seen to be paired and there is much excited courtship, with paired females attacking other females that approach closely. Among the red (and northern) phalaropes the males do the incubating, and the females take the initiative in courtship, and it is not unusual to see several females pursuing one male. Coition takes place on the water. The great air of frenzied activity, which is so prevalent where large numbers of phalaropes are gathered together like this, is very largely due to their habit of spinning rapidly round and round on the surface. This is generally considered to be a feeding activity, the spinning having the effect of stirring up bottom-living organisms. In these Arctic tundra pools it undoubtedly also serves to induce movement among the abundant mosquito larvae which must be an important item in the diet of these and other waders. However, it is quite clear from my observations that this spinning is also used on occasions as part of the courtship display. Occasionally a whole mass of phalaropes will rise up and fly rapidly round for a few moments before settling again. There is usually no apparent reason for these 'panics'. On the last day of May 1971 at Prudhoe Bay, a snowy owl flew low over the tundra and passed close to a pool occupied by a number of red phalaropes. Almost forty phalaropes rose in a mass and pursued the owl for a quarter of a mile.

As the tundra, brown and dead looking, comes into view with the melting of the snow, we hear the clear whistling notes of the golden plover (*Pluvialis dominica*) and the black-bellied or grey plover (*Squatarola squatarola*) who waste very little time in establishing the boundaries of their breeding territories. It is not very long before the tundra begins to turn green, but even before this becomes general some wild flowers are making their appearance. Around Prudhoe Bay one of the earliest to appear is the purple mountain saxifrage (*Saxifraga oppositifolia*), followed fairly rapidly by the mat-like white flowers of *Dryas integrifolia*. Further inland towards the base of the Brooks Range, the yellow flowers of glacier avens (*Geum glaciale*) push up through the melting snow on dry tundra and stony slopes, to be followed not so very much later by the delicate white flowers of the northern wind-flower (*Anemone parviflora*) whose petals have a blue tinge on the underside near the base.

The Arctic summer can be very short and it may, and often does, snow at any time. It can be well into June on the Arctic Slope before the thaw is completed, and it may begin to freeze again in September. Conditions such as these impose certain problems for both the plants and animals that live in such an environment. The growing season for plants in some areas may be as short as four to five weeks and during this time they must complete the cycle of growth and reproduction. Many Arctic plants reproduce by means of vegetative growth rather than seed production. Many of the birds must begin to breed soon after their arrival in the area. Ducks and geese, in particular, must do this, since both adults and young have to complete a summer moult before they are ready to fly out at the onset of the freeze-up. I have seen Canada and white-fronted geese sitting on full clutches completely surrounded by snow and in fluctuating temperatures that may drop well below freezing point. On the cliffs above the Sagavanirktok River a pair of peregrine falcons (*Falco peregrinus*) had three eggs in a nest in deep snow on a bluff. The early onset of cold weather in late summer can cause heavy mortality among young waterfowl and loons.

Let us look at one or two of the peculiarities of the Arctic tundra ecosystem, which is subject to biological oscillations very largely imposed by annual oscillations of environmental factors. The probability of snow in any period of the summer has already been mentioned, and related to this are large fluctuations in temperature from day to day. The time interval required for temperature changes to take place is remarkably small, often being only a matter of hours. A typical rapid temperature change occurred in June 1970 when, in the course of a back-packing trip in the Brooks Range, Pete Martin of Anchorage and myself arrived in the Ribdon Valley. The Ribdon River is an eastern tributary of the Sagavanirktok River some 106 miles or so south of the

The long-tailed jaeger or skua nests on the tundra and preys to a considerable extent upon rodents. In years when these are scarce the jaegers may not nest at all.

Arctic Ocean. It was hot and sunny when we reached the Ribdon, the temperature being about 60°F. An hour or two later the thermometer had dropped to around 45°F, the wind had risen to screaming pitch and our small tent was lashed by huge hailstones. Three hours later when the storm had finally passed we emerged to a greatly changed scene. The dry hummocks around the tent had been bright with the ground-hugging blooms of moss campion (*Silena acaulis*) and Siberian phlox (*Phlox sibirica*) when we first arrived. Now there were none, their petals had been smashed by the hail. Another example of drastic temperature change occurred at Prudhoe Bay in late June 1971 when the thermometer actually reached 70°F during brilliant sunshine, only to drop to around 40°F seventy-two hours later when fog and cloud rolled in off the Arctic Ocean.

The populations of some of the tundra mammals, as mentioned earlier, oscillate on a more or less regular, cyclic basis. The most notable of these mammals are the lemmings, in particular the brown lemmings (*Lemmus trimucronatus*). Lemming populations normally fluctuate on a four-year cycle which is closely r lated to the productivity and quality of the tundra vegetation which varies from year to year, partly as a result of climatic conditions. Obviously these fluctuations in the rodent populations influence the numbers of local predators in whose diet they form an important item. On the Arctic Slope these predators are chiefly the snowy owl, the rough-legged hawk or buzzard (*Buteo lagopus*), the pomarine jaeger or skua (*Stercorarius pomarinus*), the long-tailed jaeger or skua (*S. longicaudus*) and the Arctic fox. Overall, these climatic and biological oscillations result in a somewhat unstable situation which is frequently expressed by references to the 'fragile ecology' of the tundra. It may be added that the numbers of willow ptarmigan also fluctuate greatly at times for reasons that are not entirely clear. The situation is complicated further by the fact that the Arctic Slope populations are migratory, and the great majority (but by no means all) move southwards through Anaktuvuk Pass and other valleys in the Brooks Range to winter on the south side of the mountains down as far as the Koyukuk River. It has been estimated that something in the order of 50,000 willow ptarmigan may migrate back and forth through Anaktuvuk Pass annually. The fall movement to the south normally commences in late September and reaches a peak in mid-October. The return movement northwards appears to have two phases: some pass through towards the end of January and in February, but the main movement occurs in April. The Nunamiut Eskimos of Anaktuvuk Pass are so familiar with these two very distinct late winter and spring movements to the north that they have given separate names of 'Iklit' and 'Kadgiliotit' respectively to each migration.

Returning to the tundra itself, the many interesting and peculiar features of the Arctic Slope are revealed with the disappearance of the winter snow cover. Seen from a distance or from the air the tundra has the appearance of a smooth green meadow. That this is pretty well a total illusion becomes painfully evident on close acquaintance, particularly when one has to traverse on foot an extensive area of cottongrass tussock tundra. There are of course various types of tundra and as one proceeds south from the shore of the Arctic Ocean the flat and water-logged coastal plain gives way to rolling foothills and escarpments with dry tundra, and then to the plateaus and montane tundra of the Brooks Range. The change from sea level to the high alpine habitat is reflected clearly in the fauna and flora. We find the willow ptarmigan replaced by the rock ptarmigan (*Lagopus mutus*) from about 3,000 feet, and the peregrine falcon replaced by the gyrfalcon (*Falco rusticolus*) which, in the Brooks Range, nests from around the 2,000 foot contour upwards. At the higher altitudes we also encounter the horned lark (*Eremophila alpestris*) and the wheatear (*Oenanthe oenanthe*) which are not normally seen out on the low-lying tundra. Striking differences in the vegetation are obvious and, passing through the zone of alpine species such as the mountain avens (*Dryas octopetala*), one comes eventually to a zone where only lichens and bare rocks remain.

A bird's eye view of the coastal plain in summer reveals a number of interesting physical features. Almost the entire Arctic Slope is underlain by continuous permafrost which, as a result of drilling for oil, is now known to extend downwards in some places for as much as 2,000 feet. This permanently frozen ground is overlain by a shallow stratum of soil and vegetation known as the active layer, which varies from being a few inches deep in some places to as much as five feet in others. This is all that thaws out in the summer. The active layer is in fact a very effective insulating blanket protecting the surface of the permafrost from the melting influence of the sun. The permanently frozen ground makes it impossible for water to drain into the ground, with the result that on the relatively level plain it lies on the surface to form a myriad of lakes, pools and waterlogged tundra. A glance at the photogrammetric maps of the Arctic Slope shows that in some areas, notably west of the Colville River, standing water may occupy up to eighty per cent of the surface area.

Also noticeable is a curious pattern covering wide areas of the surface of the ground. This frequently takes the form of large polygons and the ground is referred to scientifically as polygonal-patterned ground.

*Left* Unlike several other Arctic mammals, the red fox, whose range extends well north on to the Arctic Slope, does not assume a white coat in winter.

*Above* A red fox cub waits at the entrance to the den for the vixen to return with prey.

What causes this patterning? The explanation is in fact fairly simple, at least in so far as the basic principles are concerned. In winter the tundra shrinks in the intense cold and cracks along planes of weakness. These cracks become filled with soil and ice and then the thaw commences and the warmth of summer causes the tundra to expand, the resulting pressure forcing the edges of the cracks into ridges. When the thaw is complete the ground inside the ridges is flooded with water and we have the pattern of standing water and dividing ridges so characteristic of much of the Arctic tundra. This phenomenon is not of course confined to Arctic Alaska but is found under similar conditions on tundra all round the pole.

It should perhaps be mentioned that once formed, an area of polygons assumes a regular and stable pattern. However, there are many stages in both the formation and ageing of polygons, so that the traveller over the tundra will find many variations on the general theme, but this is not the place to discuss the detailed geomorphology. The polygonal ridges are very interesting from the natural history point of view and will be discussed further later in the book.

When Vilhalmur Stefansson and the Eskimos were dog sledging across the Arctic Slope from Barrow in the west to Barter Island in the east, the only objects that they would have seen rising sharply above the level of the coastal plain were the pingos. In point of fact, pingos held the monopoly in this respect until the quite recent arrival of early warning stations and drilling rigs on the Arctic scene. The name pingo was, I believe, originated by the Eskimos of the lower Mackenzie basin in Canada, but it is now in general use. Pingos are fascinating and have considerable ecological importance. There are quite a few scattered over the Arctic Slope and I have examined a number between the Kavik River and the Kuparuk River. Pingos vary in shape and size but on average reach 39 to 82 feet in height and 98 to 197 feet in width, although very large pingos may be as much as 164 feet in height. In outline they may present an unbroken dome, or the top may have collapsed to form a crater which is frequently filled with water. They vary also in structure and many have as a core a mass of pure ice. There are at least two main processes by which pingos are formed. One form of pingo, usually referred to as the East Greenland type, is associated with the formation or expansion of gaps in the permafrost. Here, the ascension of subpermafrost water and gas under hydrostatic pressure produces massive ice formation and updoming, usually with a centrally-located area of weakness in which crater formation occurs. This type of pingo may sometimes occur in groups. The second sort of pingo, known as the Mackenzie type, is normally found on former lake floors where its formation is initiated by the contraction of gaps in the permafrost. As the gap closes the ensuing increase in volume associated with freezing causes a vertical ascent of water and fine sediments in a comparatively narrow channel. A mound gradually forms under the lake and grows until the lake is eventually sucked dry. At its final stage of maximum growth the pingo is then surrounded by a dry lake bed. It is also worth remembering that pingos are not necessarily permanent and may disappear in the course of time. They should not be confused with earth hummocks and frost boils, which are in any case much smaller in size.

One of the first pingos that I examined in detail was a reasonably large one on the coastal plain between the Sagavanirktok River and the Toolik River, just a few miles west of the Franklin Bluffs, which are the last high ground in the Sagavanirktok Valley before the Arctic Ocean is reached. This was at the end of July and it was obvious that this particular pingo had been used for some time as a plucking post by

The pingo, one of the few objects rising above the level expanse of the Arctic coastal tundra, is an important habitat for plants and animals.

a bird of prey, almost certainly the immature golden eagle (*Aquila chrysaetos*) that was seen in the vicinity. Scattered over the top of the pingo were numerous pellets containing the remains of willow ptarmigan and Arctic ground squirrels (*Citellus undulatus*). There was a sizeable colony of ground squirrels in this pingo, and they are of course abundant on the Arctic Slope and indeed over much of Alaska up to quite considerable elevations in the mountains. Numerous though they are on the Arctic Slope, the local distribution is governed to a very large extent by permafrost and drainage. They must have a reasonable depth of ice-free substratum in which to burrow and freedom from the danger of flooding under normal conditions. Obviously pingos are ideal habitats in this respect, particularly as they often have quite a considerable depth of soil. When surprised, ground squirrels almost invariably 'freeze' in the upright position, supported by the tail which is pressed flat to the ground behind, before vanishing down their burrows.

Judging by the great lumps of tundra that had been torn up at one place on this pingo, a grizzly bear (*Ursus arctos*) had been endeavouring to dig out squirrels, something that I was to observe for myself on subsequent occasions elsewhere. Quite often the bear expends considerable effort to no avail, since the squirrel, unless it has gone into a dead-end burrow, frequently escapes. The ground squirrel, numerous as it is, is an important link in the Arctic food chain. In addition to the golden eagle and grizzly already mentioned, they are preyed upon by both red foxes (*Vulpes fulva*) and Arctic foxes which take large numbers of them, and also by the wolf (*Canis lupus*) which will hunt them in the absence of larger prey.

In September 1969 I was once again in the area west of Franklin Bluffs looking, among other things, at pingos. One visited on this occasion had a considerable growth of scrub willow on the slopes and peering into these bushes I found myself literally eyeball to eyeball with an Arctic fox cub that had curled up there and gone to sleep. A beautiful dark silver-grey in colour, it did not seem greatly perturbed at this sudden intrusion and ran off a short distance before curling up in another nook, from whence it kept a beady eye on subsequent proceedings. There was no sign of a fox den on this pingo which was about forty-five miles south of the coast. On this part of the Arctic Slope, most of the Arctic fox dens that I have seen have been close to the coast, as for example on the sand dunes near the mouth of the Sagavanirktok River.

Almost immediately after this encounter with the young fox we spotted a short-tail weasel or ermine (*Mustela erminea*) in the grass. It came out of one squirrel burrow, bounded along for a few yards and disappeared down another hole. It was noticeable because it was in the pure white winter pelage with a black tip on the tail, although there was as yet no snow on the tundra. In the course of the next half an hour there ensued a game of hide and seek in an effort to photograph this implacable enemy of the ground squirrel. One hesitates to anthropomorphize the behaviour of animals but on occasions it becomes difficult to avoid doing so. This was one such occasion and I am convinced that that weasel was deliberately playing a game. At one stage I had my gaze (and the camera lens) fixed on the mouth of a burrow from which I anticipated it would emerge, only to look down and find that it had come out of a hole between my feet and was standing upright with its front paws on the toe of my boot, its tiny black eyes fixed on mine with an unwavering gaze for just an instant before it vanished again. Within a mile or so of this pingo a total of eight other Arctic foxes were seen out on the tundra, all in the white coat of winter and therefore quite conspicuous.

43

Travelling across the tundra towards another pingo we noticed, through field glasses, a number of birds circling around something at its base. On arrival we found the remains of a caribou which, judging from one or two scats and other signs, had been killed within the past day or so by wolves. Cleaning up what had been left by the original predators were no less than eighteen short-eared owls (*Asio flammeus*). This was at 3.30 p.m. one afternoon. When I returned to the spot the following morning at 9 a.m. only one owl was to be seen in the vicinity. The appearance of so many of these owls at one spot is rather interesting, particularly since in that year (1969) I had seen only one previously, and that was in July and some twenty miles further south. It is certainly far from a common breeding species on the Arctic Slope and these eighteen must have been drawn from a wide area. The question is were they brought together simply by the presence of the carrion, or had they in fact flocked together in preparation for the fall migration to the south?

The soil and vegetation covering the surface of pingos is virtually an extension of that of the surrounding tundra, although often much better drained. In fact some pingos have a very considerable depth of soil covering them. However, one is likely to find on them some flowers that will be absent or rare on the surrounding tundra, particularly if that is of the waterlogged type characterized by sedges. On one pingo near the Kuparuk River, for instance, in early June I found *Dryas integrifolia,* in considerable quantity, purple mountain saxifrage (a different form from that found in the mountains), alpine milk vetch (*Astralagus alpinus*), black oxytrope (*Oxytropis nigrescens*), northern buttercup (*Ranunculus pedatifidus*), woolly lousewort (*Pedicularis kanei*), a white species of *Draba* (one of the mustard family), Arctic poppy (*Papaver macounii*) and the boreal Jacob's ladder (*Polemonium boreale*). I

The short-tail weasel or ermine, here seen in its winter coat, is an inveterate enemy of the Arctic ground squirrel.

44

was interested to note that in the great majority of cases the latter flower was growing around the entrances to ground squirrel burrows.

There do not seem to be any birds that have a particular association with pingos, but in June 1971 I consistently saw a pair of buff-breasted sandpipers (*Tryngites subruficollis*) on one near Prudhoe Bay. This pair was on several occasions seen displaying, and one particular action in which one wing was raised vertically, and then vibrated rapidly, was most attractive. There is little doubt in my mind that a pair or so of these sandpipers were breeding in the Prudhoe Bay area, and I believe that a nest was in fact found after my visit. This is interesting as it was generally believed that on the Arctic Slope the buff-breasted sandpiper bred only in the Barrow area. However, even more interesting has been the appearance in the Prudhoe Bay area in early June of one or two stilt sandpipers, a species that has never been proved to breed on the Arctic Slope. It is probable that they are simply migrants on their way east to the Mackenzie area in Canada where it is known that they nest, or to Barter Island off the north-east coast of Alaska, where they have been reported to nest. Even close to the Arctic Ocean redpolls (*Acanthis flammea*) will be found feeding on pingos that have a growth of dwarf birch (*Betula nana*) or willows. To the biologist, of course, pingos are very useful. On the flat tundra they offer a fine vantage point from which to examine the surrounding areas. In fact the view from an average sized pingo is roughly equivalent to that from the deck of a small ship at sea.

Descending, however, to ground level once again we can examine the extensive areas of sedge-grass marsh that dominate much of the tundra. As the name implies the vegetation here consists of sedges, but there are also many species of moss and flowers such as the tall louse-wort (*Pedicularis sudetica*), the grained saxifrage (*Saxifraga foliolosa*), the bog rosemary (*Andromeda polifolia*), with its little pink balls, and the sweet coltsfoot (*Petasites frigidus*). The roots of the latter plant are roasted and eaten by the Siberian Eskimo. In this habitat there is normally an inch or so of standing water through which one can slosh along quite confidently, since the underlying permafrost provides a firm support. These shallow marshes are the feeding ground for many waders, such as the long-billed dowitcher (*Limnodromus scolopaceus*), and pectoral and semi-palmated sandpipers.

The areas of sedge-grass marsh are usually divided up by a fine network of small raised peaty ridges, which have quite a characteristic floral community with species such as dwarf birch, bearberry (*Arctostaphylos alpina*), Bering chickweed (*Cerastium beeringianum*), tall Jacob's ladder (*Polemonium acutiflorum*), valerian (*Valeriana capitata*), bog saxifrage (*Saxifraga hirculus*) and marsh fivefinger (*Potentilla palustris*), although the last two species may also be found growing in standing water on the flats. It is worth mentioning in passing that tea can be made from the dried leaves of the marsh fivefinger. I have not myself tried this, although I have made tea with the leaves of the Labrador tea plant (*Ledum palustre*) which is widespread throughout Alaska. On these raised ridges will be found the nests of sandpipers, such as the pectoral and semi-palmated, and occasionally those of the red phalarope, although this species commonly constructs its nest at the edge of standing water. We can also find the nests of ducks such as old-squaw and eider. The geese seem to prefer drier and somewhat higher ground on which to nest, while whistling swans normally seek an island or hummock surrounded by water of reasonable depth.

One of the characteristic features of the tundra at the beginning of summer is the display flights and songs of the various waders. In the vicinity of Prudhoe Bay one of the most numerous waders is the semi-palmated sandpiper. These birds indulge in display flights where one or more individuals fly upwards to quite a good height and then glide downwards with the wings held a few degrees above the horizontal and rapidly 'shivered' as they descend. All the time the air is full of their loud trilling calls. Not infrequently two of these sandpipers will indulge in a chase over a wide area. Flying low and very fast and often joined by other individuals until half a dozen or more are flashing round, they twist, turn and dive in unison to the accompaniment of excited calls. Then there are the displays of Baird's sandpiper (*Erolia bairdii*) where the male follows the female closely, flying a little above and behind with fast erratic wing beats. In the Ribdon River valley I saw four of these birds, presumably two pairs, indulge in a fast line-astern pursuit flight low over the tundra for a mile or more.

The distribution of the various species of sandpiper and other waders on the Arctic Slope is not by any means uniform. From about the Sagavanirktok River in the east to the Colville River in the west, the semi-palmated sandpiper is most numerous in the coastal area, and as one proceeds inland it is replaced by Baird's sandpiper which prefers raised ground and drier conditions for nesting. On the other hand, other species, such as the pectoral sandpiper and golden plover, are fairly generally distributed from the coast to the foothills. Then there are species whose status is not well known. In June 1970, I was excited to find, on dry tundra in the Ribdon River valley, no less than nine pairs of least sandpipers (*Erolia minutilla*) displaying and holding territory and I was even more excited to find a nest. It was clear that laying had just begun and at the time I thought I had obtained the first evidence of breeding by this species on the Arctic Slope. However, I was subsequently informed by Dr Tom Cade that he had found nests further north and east in the vicinity of Peters Lake and Schrader Lake. Nevertheless, it is plainly a species that does not commonly breed in this general area and much remains to be learnt about its distribution there.

All through the summer when the tundra is a vast and limitless expanse of green, relieved by the waving white heads of the fluffy cottongrass and clumps of bright yellow poppies, there is one small bird that can hardly be missed. Occurring all the way from the mountains to the coast, the Lapland longspur or Lapland bunting (*Calcarius lapponicus*) is perhaps the most common small bird in North America, and on the tundra its musical outpourings, delivered during a song flight, are a notable contribution to the atmosphere of these great open spaces. One can no more envisage the tundra without the Lapland longspur than the English downs and fields without the skylark. I have found a number of nests of this longspur, and they have all been built into the side of a tussock of cottongrass. I once spent three hours lying within seven feet of a nest in full view of the birds. The male would not come near but the female, oblivious to my presence, returned to feed the four young every five to seven minutes, her beak full of daddy longlegs and spiders. About every fourth or fifth visit she would remove the faecal sacs from the nest as she left.

Also occurring on the Arctic Slope is another species of longspur, Smith's longspur (*Calcarius pictus*), which is far less numerous than the one just mentioned. The male in breeding plumage is resplendent in rich buff (sometimes almost orange) with a striking black and white facial pattern. To see this longspur one has to roam the valleys of the Brooks Range foothills, valleys such as those of the Atigun, Anaktuvuk and Sagavanirktok Rivers, and in particular valleys where there are areas of sedge-grass marsh in the valley bottoms. The spatial ranges of the two species of longspur overlap in these foothills, but they nest in quite different situations. The Lapland longspur likes dry conditions provided by well drained areas of tussock tundra and ridges, while Smith's longspur inhabits the waterlogged sedge-grass areas. Nests of the latter species that I have examined were built in isolated tussocks and were lined with a few ptarmigan feathers. While I rested by a small lake at about 2,600 feet on the south side of the Atigun Canyon one afternoon in late June, the melodious warbler-like song of a Smith's longspur was the only sound disturbing the silence.

The Continental Divide of the Brooks Range is the source of numerous rivers that flow northwards towards the Arctic Ocean, and the largest drainage system north of these mountains is that of the Colville River. Several sizeable rivers flow into the Colville, including the Chandler and the Anaktuvuk. The Colville itself is a large and powerful river with an extensive delta area, while further in towards the mountains it is overlooked by a succession of high bluffs. From Umiat north along the west side of the river are a string of bluffs with resounding names such as Tattitgak Bluff, Shivugak Bluff, Uluksrak Bluff, Ishukpak Bluff, and Sentinel Hill. These and other commanding heights provide nesting sites for the peregrine falcon, gyrfalcon and rough-legged hawk, the latter being perhaps the most numerous bird of prey to be found on the Arctic Slope. Upriver from Umiat the Colville bends westwards and receives many small rivers, such as the Killik, Kurupa, Etivluk and Ipnavik, flowing down from the mountains to the south. Generally speaking, the rivers from the Colville westwards flow northwards through incised valleys, while those to the east of the Colville broaden out as they leave the mountains to form wide braided valleys with numerous gravel bars and terraces. The northern foothill

In this striking picture a female wolf feeds a cub.

country of the Brooks Range is in fact a living geological and geographic text book, exhibiting a rugged relief with irregular buttes, mesas, ridges and undulating tundra. Flying north-east from Anaktuvuk Pass, for instance, one passes over an area with some really classic anticlines.

I have had the good fortune to spend hundreds of hours exploring the valleys and foothills from the Anaktuvuk and Colville Rivers in the west eastwards to the Arctic National Wildlife Range, of which more will be said later. It is a wonderful experience to wander along these valleys and across the intervening hills, physically exhausting but emotionally stimulating. Sudden violent storms form in the mountains as giant thunderheads over the high peaks, and roll out over the foothills to deluge the traveller with torrential rain or hail for a short while; and for a few weeks in summer millions of mosquitoes do their best to drive one mad. However such events are more than compensated for by the beauty of the scenery, the ever-changing cloud formations, the peace and tranquillity, the incredible soft light of the sun in the early hours of a June morning, the weird cries of Arctic loons or black-throated divers (*Gavia arctica*) floating on glassy-surfaced lakes, or the distant mournful howling of a wolf. All these things combine to produce the unique atmosphere of Arctic Alaska. Such surroundings bring to mind the words of R. W. Emerson who wrote 'Give me a day with nature and I will make the pomp of Emperors ridiculous.'

The wide braided valleys of these Arctic Slope rivers provide a study in themselves: here one can see plants and animals that are not characteristic of the surrounding expanses of tundra. Many of these valleys have substantial thickets of willow, alder (*Alnus crispa*), and dwarf birch, and sometimes there are balsam poplars too. As one proceeds northwards these thickets become sparse and stunted, but they provide a habitat for small birds such as the redpoll, the tree sparrow (*Spizella arborea*) and the savannah sparrow (*Passerculus sandwichensis*). In some places the river banks in summer are gay with flowers such as the alpine shooting star (*Dodecatheon frigidum*), the pale paintbrush (*Castilleja caudata*), the large-flowered wintergreen (*Pyrola grandiflora*), the Arctic lupine (*Lupinus arcticus*) and shrubs such as the Lapland rosebay (*Rhododendron lapponicum*) and Labrador tea. Thus the innumerable shades of green are studded with the brighter colours, white, blue, yellow, red and purple, of these flowers. Some of the flowers are of particular interest. For instance, the Alaska boykinia or Richardson's saxifrage (*Boykinia richardsonii*), growing up to three feet in height with a spike of red-centred creamy flowers, is considered to be a relic from the Tertiary period. It is found only in Alaska and a small area of Arctic Canada.

Many of the gravel bars are colonized by a variety of flowers, including river beauty (*Epilobium latifolium*) and Eskimo potato (*Hedysarum alpinum*), the petals of which provide two contrasting shades of purple, one light and the other dark. Also, among the large stones, one may find the tight yellow cushion of the alpine hawksbeard (*Crepis nana*) or the trailing white flowers of merckia (*Wilhelmsia physodes*). Although it can be found on gravel bars close to the Arctic Ocean, the alpine hawksbeard occurs southwards into the mountains up to 6,500 feet above sea level. The Eskimo or Indian potato, as the name implies, was used by the natives as an item of food, the roots and young stems being edible. Sometimes known also as bear root, it is much sought after by the grizzly when it emerges from its winter sleep, and at this time one can see them digging for the roots out on the river flats. This raises an interesting point. Also found on gravel bars of the Arctic Slope is a very similar species, the wild sweet pea (*Hedysarum mackenzii*) which is said to be poisonous. The question is, does the grizzly distinguish between the roots of these two species, and if so how?

Characteristic breeding birds of the gravel bars are the Arctic tern (*Sterna paradisea*), the glaucous gull (*Larus hyperboreus*), the semi-palmated plover (*Charadrius semipalmatus*) and the spotted sandpiper (*Actitis macularia*). The terns often form small scattered colonies, while on some offshore islands the gull may breed in quite large colonies, but it is normally a solitary nester, breeding inland along the river valleys, well into the foothills. Nests of the glaucous gull have been found for example at Anaktuvuk Pass and in the upper reaches of the Colville River. A scavenger and predator, very little comes amiss to this gull. In July 1969 I watched two of them trying to grap a pintail duck from the surface of a lake. They spent nearly five minutes at this, their mode of attack being to take turns in diving down to approach the duck low over the water from the rear. As one gull rose from its swoop the other commenced its dive. The duck evaded capture by diving beneath the surface at the last moment with a great splash, and eventually the gulls gave up the attack. A short time after witnessing this episode I saw a single gull attempting to take young greater scaups by the same method.

Most glaucous gull nests that I have found were on areas of relatively bare gravel on isolated bars, but a few were built on top of isolated tussocks. The normal clutch for this species is two to three eggs, but in 1970 I found a total of a dozen or so nests in the Ivishak and Sagavanirktok Valleys, most of which had what proved to be complete clutches of only one egg. Now the rodent populations in that area were at a low ebb at the time, and perhaps this was the reason for the small clutches since the glaucous gull does prey on lemmings and voles to some extent. However, it is by no means such an obligatory predator of these animals as certain other birds, such as the pomarine jaeger and the snowy owl. It is perhaps of some significance that at the same time, on rolling tundra in the valley of the Lupine River which is an eastern tributary of the Sagavanirktok, three pairs of long-tailed jaegers were defending territories but were not nesting. We watched them spend long periods quartering the tundra slopes for prey with very little success. Failure to nest or the production of smaller than normal clutches is well known among such predators when their prey is in short supply. In the fall of 1969 I was watching a flock of fifteen glaucous gulls feeding on the entrails of a caribou. A solitary gyrfalcon was circling around in the vicinity, and every time a gull flew off the falcon would dive at it repeatedly, apparently in an effort to make the gull drop whatever it might be carrying. One gull did drop a length of intestine, but caught it again before reaching the ground, where it landed and remained until the falcon had flown off. Wherever there is carrion one can be certain that ravens too will gather, and more often than not glaucous gulls also.

My first introduction to life on the tundra in a good lemming year came in the summer of 1971. In that year the numbers of brown and collared lemmings (*Dicrostonyx groenlandicus*) on the western Arctic Slope around Barrow were very high, although they had not, apparently, reached one of the cyclical 'peaks'. Large areas of tundra were covered by a network of runs and tunnels made by the lemmings. As one trod on a tussock a lemming would often rush out and shoot off along one of the runs, for all the world like a locomotive on a toy railway, disappearing into tunnels through the tussocks and emerging at high speed on the other side.

Ready to take advantage of this harvest of rodents were the snowy

*Above* As summer approaches in the High Arctic of Alaska, snow geese are among the millions of waterfowl that fly north to breed.

*Centre* The yellow-billed loon or white-billed diver, a study in black and white, is the rarest of the three species of loon that nest regularly on the Arctic Slope.

*Below* In the years when lemming populations are at a low level, snowy owls are rare or absent on the Arctic tundra. The presence of three dead brown lemmings on the rim of the nest indicates that these young snowy owls will not go short of food.

*Opposite above* Among the most beautiful of the Arctic nesting gulls is Sabine's gull.

*Opposite below* The Arctic tern, which commonly nests in northern Alaska, is one of the greatest long-distance migrants in the world.

owls and pomarine jaegers. The latter were nesting and many of the pairs were extremely aggressive, mercilessly mobbing anyone crossing their territories. One pair was particularly vicious and had developed the tactic of splitting up to attack intruders, one approaching from the rear and the other from the front. But it was really the snowy owls that dominated the scene, and on one occasion I had thirty-seven in view at one time within a field of vision of 180 degrees from a single vantage point. One nest examined contained eight young of varying size from very large to very small, and on the rim of the nest were the corpses of several brown lemmings and one collared lemming. While photographing these young owls at close quarters I was attacked by the female of the pair: she came in from above and behind and her talons ripped the back of my jacket. If some sixth sense had not made me duck it would have been my scalp that her talons had ripped.

Every time one or other of this pair of owls left or approached the nest, which was a hollow on top of a low tundra ridge, they had to pass through the territory of one or more pairs of pomarine jaegers and they were always violently mobbed. These attacks were sometimes continued after the owl had landed at the nest, and I was amazed at the agility these huge owls displayed when jumping up, flipping over on to their backs in the air and presenting vicious talons to the attacking jaegers.

Poking about among the foothill valleys and dry rolling tundra is a fascinating experience, and one could happily spend numerous summers doing nothing else. Although I have covered extensive areas of the Brooks Range by helicopter, which is invaluable as a means of doing preliminary surveys, it is only by going in on foot that one can really absorb the wilderness atmosphere and gain an intimate acquaintance with the wildlife. Looking back through field diaries, written up daily, helps to bring to life these experiences. There is much of interest at hand all the time and one never knows quite what is going to turn up next. My most memorable experiences of back-packing in the Brooks Range are those of the summer of 1970 when, with one companion, I hiked from the headwaters of the Atigun River, through into the valley of the Sagavanirktok and then north to a point some twenty miles south of Franklin Bluffs. We made many excursions into side valleys along this route and were in the field about a month. The night before we started this trip we had flown to a temporary camp at Galbraith Lake in the Atigun Valley, and there occurred one of those stupendous storms that the Brooks Range can evoke from time to time. Thunder crashed and rolled in the mountains for hours, lowering black clouds hung in the valley and sheets of rain lashed down. At two in the morning, when the rain eased, we looked out to see a sight of great beauty. The five-foot thick ice on Galbraith Lake had partly broken up (this was the third week of June) and inky black water flowed through the open leads; beyond the lake were ominous black clouds hanging over equally black mountains, but between the lake and the base of the mountains was an expanse of deep orange tundra recently exposed by the melting snow. This area of tundra was glowing in the light of the sun that shone through the one break in the clouds, and arching sky-wards was a brilliant rainbow. It would take a better poet than I to do justice to such a scene of frightening magnificence, but what an appropriate start to our camping trip it was.

In my first summer on the Arctic Slope, in 1969, I recall walking east from our camp by a lake on the edge of the Sagavanirktok Valley, just south of its junction with the Ivishak River. After a mile or so I came to a small crystal clear stream which subsequently proved to be a tributary of the Ivishak. The banks and gravel bars of this stream, or perhaps it justified the title of a small river, were well endowed with willows, some of which reached a height of almost twelve feet. Pushing through one of these thickets I found myself on the edge of an extensive open space ringed round by willows. Here was a riot of colour: grass almost formed a meadow which was studded with blue Arctic lupines, yellow alpine arnicas (*Arnica alpina*) and the pale mauve of river beauty. Not far away, four birds sitting motionless on top of some willows proved to be a party of juvenile northern shrikes (*Lanius excubitor*) which species, on the basis of the available data, does not seem to commonly breed north of the Brooks Range. However, I have also encountered this shrike in the valleys of the Lupine River, Ivishak River, Saviukviayak River, Atigun River and Sagavanirktok River. It may in fact be fairly widespread in the foothills, but very few people are there to look for it.

Further along this stream an Arctic warbler (*Phylloscopus borealis*) was heard singing and the nest was eventually located. It contained four young, one of which was dead, and another dead youngster lay just outside it. Both adults were feeding the young with flies, mosquitoes and small green caterpillars. The nest itself was built into the face of a mossy bank and was almost invisible from above. As this stream was full of grayling (*Thymallus arcticus*) it was not surprising that one or two families of red-breasted mergansers (*Mergus serrator*) were also seen. The following summer, when I again visited this location, a robin (*Turdus migratorius*) was seen carrying food to a nest. This stream is typical of many to be found on the Arctic Slope, tucked away in the rolling tussock tundra and providing a habitat for species not found in the intervening areas.

Even more interesting was an extensive grove of very tall, mature balsam poplars or cottonwoods. We found them growing all along the side of a nameless creek on the east side of the Ivishak Valley, just north of its junction with the Saviukviayak River. I believe that these may well be the most northerly tall trees in Alaska, being only about seventy-five miles south of the Arctic Ocean. They are not, of course, the most northerly trees in the world. These, much more stunted larch, spruce and alder, are to be found in the Siberian Arctic on the shores of the Laptev Sea at latitude 73°N. In one of the tall poplars was the old hole of a woodpecker, almost certainly made by a northern three-toed woodpecker (*Picoides tridactylus*). If so, this would be the most northerly point that the species had nested in Alaska. I remember also seeing a gray jay (*Perisoreus canadensis*) at this locality. Not only are there many healthy, well developed poplars along this creek, but there is also plenty of regeneration.

Balsam poplars do of course occur at other localities in the northern foothills of the Brooks Range. There are, for instance, a number of small stands in the Ribdon River valley where they nestle at the base of the hills north of the river and almost opposite Elusive Lake, and it is in this area that I heard the song of the robin one June night. Nowhere on the north side of the mountains, however, have I seen such tall trees as those to be found near the Ivishak River. Immediately south of the Ribdon River valley is Accomplishment Creek which has its origin in a number of small icefields high in the Philip Smith Mountains. It was near the mouth of this creek in July 1970 that Dr Clayton M. White saw a black-billed magpie (*Pica pica*) which, as far as we know, is the first to have been seen north of the Brooks Range.

I have penetrated the Ribdon Valley from the river's junction with the Sagavanirktok to its source in the mountains, a distance of over forty miles. Close to the upper end of the valley one can get over a fairly low pass into the headwaters of the Lupine River. Both these

*Overleaf* In the Ribdon River valley in the northern foothills of the Brooks Range, Elusive Lake nestles at the foot of mountains dusted with the fresh snow of September. *Inset left* Early May in the central Brooks Range, an endless snow-covered vista of razor-backed ridges and jagged peaks. *Inset right* High summer on the Arctic tundra. A sea of waving white cottongrass provides a foreground to shimmering lakes and distant mountains. The wilderness atmosphere of these vast open spaces is emphasized by the weird cries of loons on the tundra lakes.

A cow moose in the forest. The strictly herbivorous moose is common throughout most of Alaska.

rivers are usually rather dry in their upper reaches once the thaw has finished as they are not fed by icefields. Very little in the way of wild-life was seen in the headwater regions of the Lupine or Ribdon, although I do remember encountering a bull moose (*Alces alces*) within half a mile of the source of the latter. The animal could not have negotiated the hills at that point and would have been forced to retrace its steps down the valley. On another occasion a group of seven Dall sheep (*Ovis dalli*) were seen at an elevation of 3,500 feet about fourteen miles east of Elusive Lake.

The Alaskan race of the moose is the largest and it is widely distributed from the extreme south-east right up to the Arctic Slope in the north. Biologically speaking the moose is a relatively recent arrival on the Arctic Slope and its spread has been reasonably well documented. The Nunamiut Eskimos of the Brooks Range were not familiar with it north of the mountains until about 1880, and it is on record that an occasional individual was killed along the Colville River and elsewhere from 1880 to 1900. The Colville is now one of the best areas for moose on the Arctic Slope and it has been said that the density there is comparable to that in good moose habitat further south in the taiga areas. It is significant that this animal was not mentioned at all by white travellers on the Arctic Slope during the early decades of the present century.

It is known that moose reached the Arctic Slope from south of the Brooks Range, having come through suitable passes such as those of the Chandalar, John and Kuparuk Rivers. I think it is reasonable to correlate this northward spread with the increase in mean winter temperatures in high latitudes which took place in the latter half of the nineteenth century, and which allowed a northward extension in the range of certain species of tall willows which provide good moose browse. At the present time moose can be seen almost anywhere on the Arctic Slope, even to within sight of the Arctic Ocean. I have in fact seen cows with calves within a few miles of the coast.

From the observations of petroleum exploration personnel in the late 1950s and early 1960s, and from an examination of old and recently taken aerial photographs, it is evident that willows have spread north along many of the river valleys towards the sea, and that these valley thickets have increased in both height and density in many places within recent decades. Consequently the moose has flourished on the Arctic Slope and the population is now fully self supporting and does not have to rely on immigration from the south. The moose is not the

Head held high, a bull moose runs from a bear in a river valley on Alaska's Arctic Slope.

*Right* A predator on the tundra. An Arctic ground squirrel falls prey to a red fox.

*Below* In the thick white fur of winter, an Arctic fox curls up in the snow.

*Above* Ever alert to danger, an Arctic ground squirrel sits upright for a clearer view.

*Left* The attractively marked collared lemming feeds on tundra grasses. Lemmings and voles are important links in the Arctic food chain.

only species that has colonized and spread across the Arctic Slope: the red fox has done likewise and now overlaps the range of the Arctic fox. In this case too, the amelioration of the climate has no doubt had much to do with it.

The best places to look for moose are in the river valleys, particularly those with well developed willow thickets such as one finds along the Colville River. I have come across quite high numbers of moose in valleys other than the Colville Valley. Away to the east for instance, a total of eighteen were found in early May in one small area at the junction of Eagle Creek and the Ikiakpuk River with the Canning River. A similar number was seen, again in early May, in the Ivishak Valley, among the balsam poplars and willow thickets that I have mentioned before. It was at this locality that I had an interesting experience with bears. I decided to check the spot again in early July to see if more or fewer moose were present. Arriving on the spot, we could not see a single moose and, while pondering this fact, we suddenly noticed three adult grizzlies, and a few moments later two more. Little wonder there were no moose about! I have never before or since seen so many adult grizzlies in close proximity anywhere on the Arctic Slope.

Another good moose area is the Toolik River valley between the base of the Brooks Range and the White Hills to the north. Transects along thirty-six miles of the valley in September and May produced fifty-two and fifty-seven moose respectively. It is of interest that a count made in early October, a little over a month after the September transect, revealed the presence of only eight moose. In the intervening period the weather had deteriorated markedly and they had presumably been forced to move out of the valley by heavy snows.

I find the moose a rather amusing animal, although I would not include cows with calves in that category. One particular episode that struck me as very funny occurred in the Lupine River valley in late September. I was stalking a very large bull moose with the camera, and, unknown to me at first, a grizzly was ahead also stalking the moose. Eventually the bear became aware of my presence and rushed off at high speed passing within a few feet of the moose, swam across the river and then flopped out on a grassy hillside beyond, where it promptly went to sleep. The moose watched the precipitate flight of the bear with what must have been the nearest thing to a broad grin that any animal could achieve. In the same valley in July the following year, a cow moose came every evening to the far side of a small lake by which we were camped. She would wade out to a grassy island and settle down for the night. Our various activities were watched with an air of great interest, particularly when we were bathing in the lake. On another occasion I walked up to within eight feet of a young bull moose which totally ignored me, an indifference that has also been exhibited by larger bulls at times.

How many moose are there on the Arctic Slope? This is in fact a question that can be answered with some degree of accuracy thanks to an official census carried out in April 1970 by the Alaska Department of Fish and Game. The area covered extended from the Arctic National Wildlife Range in the east to the Colville River and its headwaters in the west, and a total of just over 1,700 moose were counted, of which approximately seventy-seven per cent were adults.

The Dall sheep, one of the species of the bighorn group, is widely distributed in the Brooks Range and I have seen these animals in many localities on both sides of the Continental Divide. What the population amounts to in total appears to be unknown. Fully mature rams with a full curl of horns are, of course, coveted trophies to the hunter. As these

*Opposite* A Dall sheep ram with a fine curl of horns rests in an alpine meadow, high in the mountains.

*Right* The creamy white flowers of mountain avens are a conspicuous feature of the Arctic Slope flora.

*Below* Aptly named the woolly lousewort, this is only one of several species of *Pedicularis* occurring on the Arctic Slope of Alaska.

*Below right* Probably a relic from the Tertiary period, Alaska boykinia or Richardson's saxifrage is only found in Alaska and a small part of Arctic Canada.

*Above left* From June to August the yellow blooms of Arctic poppies enliven the tundra.

*Above* Siberian phlox, an attractive alpine and sub-alpine species found in the Brooks Range, is highly variable in colour.

*Left* Purple mountain saxifrage is one of the earliest saxifrages to come into flower.

sheep spend most of their time at relatively high altitudes and on steep slopes, one of the characteristic sights of these mountains is to see a line of them on a high ridge, standing out white against a blue sky. Their agility in negotiating at speed the steepest slopes and the most rugged of crags is quite phenomenal. I have found it possible to approach Dall sheep closely on various occasions. The method that I found most successful is to approach from below and to move slowly and quite openly. The natural reaction of these sheep to predators is to move upwards to higher elevations where they can find safety on the crags and cliffs. It is when crossing valley floors from one mountain to another that they are most vulnerable, particularly to wolves which are their main natural enemy.

Grazing as they do on the sparse grass, mosses, lichens and leafy alpines such as the mountain avens, they require certain minerals in their diet, and for this purpose they resort to mineral licks. Once a mineral lick has been discovered the observer can lie in wait and often see quite large numbers of sheep at reasonably close quarters. One such lick that I found was near Wahoo Lake, high in the upper reaches of the Echooka River valley.

There is another way of watching large numbers of Dall sheep with the minimum expenditure of effort, and that is when they are lambing. In much the same way that caribou resort to selected areas to drop their calves, so do the sheep move to favoured lambing areas. Among the best localities known to me for watching sheep in the Brooks Range is the Atigun Canyon, which runs east-west and through which the Atigun River flows to join the Sagavanirktok. A dark and somewhat depressing area, due to the black colour of much of the terrain, it is also a natural rain trap. Nevertheless the steep slopes on each side are criss-crossed with sheep trails and during the lambing season, in late May and early June, the numbers of sheep there may exceed 300 at times. There are two prime lambing areas at opposite ends and on opposite sides of this canyon, and on the south side there are also two mineral licks.

From the reports available it seems that the sheep begin to move into the canyon area from the south in spring, numbers reach a peak at the time of lambing, movement out to the south occurs in late June, and then in August they move back into the area again. The number of adult rams in the canyon is never very high and the population there is dominated, not surprisingly, by ewes and young animals. It is a charming sight to see the ewes with their lambs scattered over the alpine pastures high above the steep sides of the canyon. The lambs are very precocious and begin grazing a few days after birth.

Despite its forbidding appearance the Atigun Canyon is an interesting place for reasons other than the presence of Dall sheep. Here, for instance, one may see the wandering tattler (*Heteroscelus incanum*), the gyrfalcon and the golden eagle. There are, in fact, two eagle eyries less than three miles apart on opposite sides of the canyon, which is pretty close for these large birds of prey. My observations indicate that they hunt over quite different areas.

It was in the course of a back-packing trip through this eight-mile-long canyon in 1970 that we made some interesting discoveries, although we had to camp for two days at the western end and watch the rain pouring down inside the canyon before we could enter it. The first thing we found were two pairs of Say's phoebes (*Sayornis saya*) nesting about four or five feet above the rushing river. This is not a common species north of the Brooks Range, although one or two instances of breeding have been noted at Anaktuvuk Pass and in the Colville River area. Even more exciting was the discovery of a colony of seven to ten pairs of cliff swallows (*Petrochelidon pyrrhonota*) on an almost vertical cliff face overlooking a tributary of the Atigun River on the south side of the canyon. Previously the only evidence of breeding by this species on the north side of the Brooks Range was provided by a colony of about a hundred nests containing mummified birds, found near the head of the Kuparuk River at the beginning of the century. A few weeks before our walk through the canyon a yellow-shafted flicker (*Colaptes auratus*) had been seen there. The remains of this flicker were found a few days later: it had very likely fallen prey to the gyrfalcon.

These ornithological discoveries in the Atigun Canyon illustrate the excitement and fascination of wandering on foot through the Brooks Range foothills. From one valley to the next one never knows what is going to reveal itself. There may be other colonies of cliff swallows in these mountain valleys, but it could be years before they are discovered. The bird life of the Anaktuvuk Pass area and the Colville River has been well studied over a long period, and I have carried out studies in the Sagavanirktok and Atigun Valleys, but hundreds of other valleys remain a closed book.

As one travels westwards from the Atigun Valley into the Endicott Mountains and then the Baird Mountains, the last high peaks in the Brooks Range are passed, peaks such as the massive block of Mount Doonerak at 7,610 feet and Alapah Mountain at 8,500 feet. Then there is Anaktuvuk Pass with its village of Nunamiut Eskimos to whom the caribou are still of great importance. Further west still towards the Bering Sea is the Arrigetch Range, an eight mile horseshoe of stupendous needle-like peaks encircling a creek which has its source in one of the few true glaciers in the Brooks Range. The Arrigetch Peaks are the only intrusion of granite in the entire Brooks Range. Much of this country, on both sides of the Continental Divide, was explored by Robert Marshall between 1929 and 1939 and is immortalized in his classic book *Alaska Wilderness* which first appeared in 1956. This is a fine and breathtakingly beautiful area of isolated peaks, high cirques and U-shaped valleys, all mute evidence of past glacial activity. I am really not able to add anything to Robert Marshall's vivid writings about this area. Back-packing through that country one becomes very conscious of the atmosphere and scenic effects that inspired Marshall's deep feelings.

If, on the other hand, we go north-east from the Atigun area across to the Canning River, we come to the incomparable 8.9 million acre wilderness forming the Arctic National Wildlife Range, whose eastern boundary is the Canadian border. The mountains run close to the Arctic Ocean, and are dominated by the highest peaks in the entire Brooks Range. These are Mount Isto at 9,050 feet, Mount Chamberlain at 9,020 feet and Mount Michelson at 8,855 feet. This vast area encompasses examples of all that is best in this Arctic Region. There is rolling tundra between the mountains and the sea where, in the foothills of the Romanzof Mountains, the caribou of the Porcupine herd have their calving grounds between the Katakturuk and Kongakut Rivers. Then there are snow-capped peaks and beetling precipices, silent valleys which awake only to the periodic noise of migrating caribou, crystal clear lakes and, in the southern section where it is warmer, due to summer winds from the Yukon River basin, the edge of the spruce and deciduous forest with meandering streams and green meadows. If a man cannot find tranquillity here he will certainly not find it elsewhere.

It is there in the Arctic National Wildlife Range that one stands a chance of seeing one of the largest grazing animals on the Arctic Slope, the musk ox. If ever an animal could be said to be perfectly adapted in every way to a harsh Arctic environment, then this is it. The musk ox evolved in one of the harshest environments in the world and at one

*Overleaf* High on an alpine pasture, three Dall sheep rams relax.

time ranged the tundra from Canada north to Greenland and eastwards to Siberia. Forced northwards by climatic changes and decimated by ruthless hunting, the musk ox soon become scarce and was in fact eliminated from its native range in Alaska by the late 1860s.

One has only to look at a musk ox in order to see its superb adaptation to a cold and exposed environment. The dense woolly fleece is both wind and snowproof and, in bad weather, they make the most of this by forming a tight group and thus reducing heat loss from the younger animals. This is in fact similar to the behaviour that they adopt in the face of a predator such as a wolf, bear or man; they form a tight defensive circle or square with the adults on the outside and the calves in the middle. This technique, which presents a ring of vicious horns to the attacker, was useless against man with his rifles. Musk oxen require hillsides and slopes that are blown fairly clear of snow so that in winter they can graze the frozen vegetation. In summer they do well on the tundra grasslands.

History is now being reversed. Musk oxen, from an introduced herd on Nunivak Island in the Bering Sea, were taken to Barter Island off the coast of the Arctic National Wildlife Range in 1969 and released there. They quickly moved across to the mainland and some were later seen as far as 150 miles to the south and 180 miles to the east in the Mackenzie area. At the present time just over twenty or so animals are known to have survived from this original transplanted group, and the best place to look for them is in the drainage area of the Sadlerochit River. In June 1970 a group of fifteen were also released at the mouth of the Kavik River some miles to the west of the Arctic National Wildlife Range, but I have no idea as to the subsequent fate or movements of this party. All being well, it may be that in a few years musk oxen will once again roam over large areas of the Arctic Slope.

The most important herbivore on the Arctic tundra is not the moose or the caribou, but the little lemming whose numbers at one of the population peaks may reach prodigious proportions. The most noticeable herbivore, however, is the barren-ground caribou. Somewhere between 380,000 and 400,000 roam the Arctic Slope in two main herds one of which, the Porcupine herd, has already been mentioned. This numbers at least 140,000 animals but the figure may in fact be as high as 170,000. These caribou winter well into the forest zone to the east and south of the Brooks Range, that is to say in the upper Porcupine River and adjacent areas. The much larger Arctic herd, which a 1970 census showed to consist of a minimum of 242,000 animals, winters south of the Brooks Range along and in the northern fringe of the

The musk ox is superbly adapted in every way to its severe environment. Here two defensive groups are formed on the snow-covered tundra. When young animals are present they are placed towards the centre of a defensive circle.

boreal forest in an area extending from the Waring Mountains and the lower Koyukuk River area eastwards to Wiseman. Their calving grounds lie north of the Brooks Range along the headwaters of the Colville, Kelik, Meade and Utukok Rivers.

Throughout the long, dark winter a few small and widely scattered groups of caribou may be found on the Arctic Slope, but it is in March or early April that the main bodies begin the journey north from the wintering grounds and come through passes in the mountains to reach the calving grounds. There the calves are usually dropped in early June. Much has been written about the great 'seas' of migrating caribou flowing over the Canadian Barrens and elsewhere, but in point of fact they do not normally move in huge compact herds. Instead, the migrating animals generally cover a wide area or occur as intermittent lines coming through mountain passes or along river valleys. Congregations of thousands do sometimes occur but these are usually transient. One example of a large gathering was a herd of 10,000 or so seen in the vicinity of Liberator Lake, near the headwaters of the Colville River in

A wolf, an important predator of the caribou, howls at the edge of the forest.

July 1969. A little later, on 20th August to be exact, a heavy concentration of about 40,000 were present on the west side of the Colville River much further north, and this probably included the total of 6,000 or so that had passed through Prudhoe Bay from the east during the preceding four or five days, heading westwards towards the Colville. In general, though, one sees them in smaller herds or groups of anything from 50 to 1,000 or more. It is towards the fall, when the bulls have joined the cows and younger animals, that the biggest concentrations are to be expected.

My finest experience of what might be termed a typical caribou migration was on 30th April, 1970, when I flew from Fairbanks in a Cessna 187, accompanied by Canadian biologist Angus Gavin. We flew north to Bettles and then up the John River valley (where we saw a black bear (*Ursus americanus*) crossing the frozen river) and over the Continental Divide into Anaktuvuk Pass. This pass is one of the major routes through the Brooks Range for migrating caribou, which is why the Nunamiut Eskimos settled there. However, we saw no caribou and so flew east to Galbraith Lake and the Atigun valley, where an attempt to get over the high pass into the head of the Dietrich Valley to the south was defeated by low cloud. It was as we were flying westwards across the mountains back to Anaktuvuk Pass that we suddenly saw a long line of caribou at about 5,000 feet. We traced their line of march back to the south until we were able to see that they were coming up the North Fork of the Koyukuk River from as far downstream as the eye could see. Flying back we found that the head of the procession had passed along Ernie Creek, past the base of Limestack Mountain, across Grayling Creek and the upper reaches of the Anaktuvuk River, then along high contours past Mount Stuver to Akvalutak Creek, from whence they debouched into the main Anaktuvuk Valley some miles north of the Eskimo village. How many caribou were there? We did not have enough time or light to find out, but between Ernie Creek and Mount Stuver alone there were at least 3,000 all moving steadily and purposefully at the 'migration trot', providing one of nature's great sights.

The caribou have several predators in addition to man, who harvests them for food. Perhaps the most traditional is the wolf, but the grizzly will also take them when opportunity offers. Wolf numbers on the Arctic Slope reached a low level as a result of the fifty dollar bounty (removed at long last in 1970) and shooting from aircraft. Happily they may now increase and perform their natural function of taking sick and weak individuals from the caribou herds. As leading Alaskan conservationist Robert Weeden has said, a land that can support the wolf is a healthy land. Most of the relatively small number of wolves that I have seen on the Arctic Slope have been solitary animals, but on 7th October, 1969, a pack of seven black wolves and one grey wolf was seen a few miles north of the White Hills, just west of the Sagavanirktok River, where it appeared to be following a caribou trail. Another occasional predator of the caribou which I have seen even less frequently is the wolverine.

An aerial view of the Arctic Slope in summer gives a distinct impression of a watery landscape for reasons that I mentioned earlier. In the northern foothills of the Brooks Range are many lakes – Lake Schrader and Lake Peters in the Arctic National Wildlife Range, Cache One Lake, Elusive Lake, Galbraith Lake, Itkillik Lake, Shainin Lake, Makaktuk Lake, Chandler Lake and many hundreds more that have no name. As one approaches the Arctic coastal plain the density of lakes increases, there being everything from large lakes to small pools. These are the feeding and breeding places for thousands of waders, ducks,

A small group of barren-ground caribou cows and yearlings runs over the snow-covered tundra.

geese, swans, and loons (divers). While large numbers of waterfowl spend the summer on the Arctic Slope, many of them are non-breeding birds which are nevertheless of great importance as reserve populations. In mid-summer packs of moulting black brants and white-fronted geese can be seen on some of the larger lakes and in river deltas.

Near the coast it will be noticed that many of these lakes are what are known as oriented lakes: the long axes lie parallel to the prevailing summer winds. Quite a few have a marginal belt of a reddish grass, called *Arctophila fulva*, in which loons frequently nest. In others the water has a reddish tinge due to the presence of ferric hydroxide. Further inland many have a richer marginal flora which includes the marsh marigold (*Caltha palustris*), buckbean and cottongrass.

Among all this wealth of waterfowl it is the loons or divers that attract me most, because it is their weird wailing and laughing cries, echoing across the otherwise silent tundra, that gives this wilderness a distinct character. There are three species of loon nesting regularly on the Arctic Slope, and they are the Arctic, red-throated (*Gavia stellata*) and yellow-billed (*G. adamsii*) loons. The first two species are common, but the third is not. To me, this yellow-billed loon is in a class of its own. It nests mostly on inaccessible lakes in the mountain foothills. With its splendid plumage it is a symphony in black and white, and the enormous ivory coloured bill makes it quite unmistakable. In three summers I found only two breeding pairs of these loons on the central Arctic Slope, and one of these was at a lake in the Ribdon River valley. Here I lay for many hours in a hollow in the tundra, screened by sprigs of willow and tormented nearly to the point of madness by hordes of mosquitoes, in order to photograph this magnificent bird at the nest. The few pictures I obtained were worth every bit of discomfort suffered.

The very embodiment of the wild spirit of the Arctic tundra is, however, without a doubt the grizzly bear. Big, beautiful, powerful and totally unpredictable this animal is fascinating to watch. Brown bears (according to current systematic thinking, the brown bears and the grizzlies are one species, *Ursus arctos*) are found throughout Alaska, but it is the sight of what is sometimes referred to as the barren-ground grizzly stalking over the open tundra north of the Brooks Range that leaves the deepest impression. He so clearly belongs there and is indisputably monarch of all he surveys with no enemy but man. Completely omnivorous, the grizzly stands at the top of the food chain in this Arctic environment.

How many grizzlies are there on the Arctic Slope? That is a question that cannot be answered with much accuracy at the present time, although studies currently under way may help to rectify the situation. There is little doubt that its density is on the low side. Detailed records were kept of all grizzlies seen in the Prudhoe Bay area and in the Sagavanirktok and Atigun River valleys from May to October 1970. A total of eighty-seven reports are considered to refer to a maximum of seventy-four individuals and probably, in fact, somewhat less than this. While this may give the impression that grizzlies are common on the Arctic Slope it must be remembered that in other areas much lower numbers were reported, and often hardly any were noted. Not surprisingly, the highest numbers of bears were seen in June, July and August. In this part of Alaska it is late April or even early May before conditions are suitable for the grizzlies to emerge from their dens in the foothills of the Brooks Range, and by late October or early November they have mostly retired again.

Due to colour or some other characteristic it was possible to recognize a certain number of individual bears and to plot their movements. A very large dark brown bear that I saw near the junction of the Ivishak and Saviukviayak Rivers on 5th June had moved fifteen miles further north by mid-July, and on 19th August was a further eleven miles to the north. So in two and a half months this one had moved only twenty-six miles from where he was first seen. Another dark individual seen out on the tundra to the west of Franklin Bluffs on 19th August had moved thirty-five miles to the south-east when seen again eleven days later, and so he had obviously been getting along quite rapidly. A number of other identifiable individuals, however, had moved less than ten miles over periods ranging from five to sixty-seven days, the latter figure referring to a sow with a cub. The records for staying put were held by a honey-blond adult that frequented a six mile stretch of the upper Atigun Valley for a period of ninety-eight days, between early June and mid-September, although it was not of course seen every day. In the same area a sow with two cubs ranged along nine miles of this valley for fifty-one days. It seems probable that many bears stay within a relatively circumscribed area if food is adequate and they are not disturbed too much.

A particularly amusing incident concerns a five year old male that took a liking to a certain camp and became quite a nuisance. Eventually it was decided that he had to go, and one July evening he was tranquillized and transported, unconscious, to the Anaktuvuk River, some ninety miles further west. Eight days later he was back at camp and as troublesome as ever. There was no possible doubt about his identity, since identifying tags had been attached to his ears before he was released.

Unfortunately I have never seen a bear kill a moose or caribou on the Arctic Slope, although I have occasionally arrived on the scene immediately afterwards. In September 1969 a very large bear was seen near Franklin Bluffs, close to the remains of a caribou on which it had c early been feeding. Although the bear was only a few yards away a flock of ravens were already clearing up some of the remains. Oddly

Impelled by the migratory urge, a large herd of barren-ground caribou traverses the wide expanse of a river valley.

enough in early September the following year, a bear was again seen on a bull caribou kill five miles west of Franklin Bluffs. A few weeks earlier, in late August, one had been spotted on a bull caribou kill by the Kuparuk River. It had eaten some of the flesh and was in the process of burying the remains when sighted. In mid-September in the upper part of the Atigun Valley, a grizzly was seen to charge a small herd of migrating caribou that were moving up the valley. It managed to divide the herd and prevented the rearmost animals from continuing up the valley for half an hour or so, but finally gave up its attempts to catch one. I imagine that most moose and caribou kills are the result of stealth and ambush rather than actual pursuit.

An interesting piece of behaviour that I observed involved a sow and two cubs that fed regularly on a dead bull moose (possibly killed by the sow) by the Sagavanirktok River, below Kakaktukruich Bluff, for several days in late September. They always fed side by side with the sow in the middle, and by the time they had finished all that was left of the moose were the antlers, a heap of skin and some large bones. The interesting thing is that when disturbed these three bears invariably retreated by climbing straight up the steep 2,800 foot bluff. On another occasion, in the Ribdon River valley, a sow with a cub was observed climbing up the steepest side of the 2,600 foot hill immediately north of Elusive Lake. They were somewhat surprised on breasting the crest to find two humans in occupation, but we decided not to dispute possession! Seeing that it was a very hot day, this climb to the top of a practically bare hill seemed rather pointless behaviour on the part of the bears, unless they were hoping for a cool breeze when they got there.

Occasionally, of course, bears become violent for no very apparent reason. I remember one particular instance that was quite hilarious. A grizzly that had been peacefully dozing on a grassy hillside for an hour, suddenly leapt up and began to run erratically backwards and forwards tearing up large chunks of tundra, and then quite suddenly calmed down and strolled off. In the summer of 1970 a helicopter had to be left unattended in the Atigun Valley for a few days, and it was pretty well bashed up by a bear, probably one that at some time or another had been annoyed by a low flying helicopter. While most grizzlies that I have met on the Arctic Slope have retreated hot foot on picking up my scent, one did charge to within a few yards before deciding that perhaps I was harmless after all. Oddly enough I did not find this experience anywhere near as disconcerting as one when a bear sat within seventy-five yards of my tent one evening while I was cooking supper. He just sat and watched and seemed to be simply curious, and it was quite some time before he finally wandered away.

Now the wind from the polar ice has been joined by the wind of change that is blowing across the tundra and through the high passes of the Brooks Range. Men, drawn by the lure of oil far below in the frozen ground, have arrived in force together with their equipment and have established residence within sight of the Arctic Ocean, where none lived permanently before. This land of limitless distances, this land that is enlivened in the short summer by the voices of myriad birds and the riot of colour of tundra flowers, that trembles to the thunder of hooves of thousands of migrating caribou, and from which emanates an atmosphere of tranquillity tempered by the knowledge that winter is always watching from the wings, this unfettered and uncontained land now faces changes greater than any since the end of the last Great Ice Age. Let us hope that whatever changes occur in the coming decades there will always be room for the grizzly and the wolf, and for the man who seeks peace of mind and somewhere from which to escape the pressures of modern life.

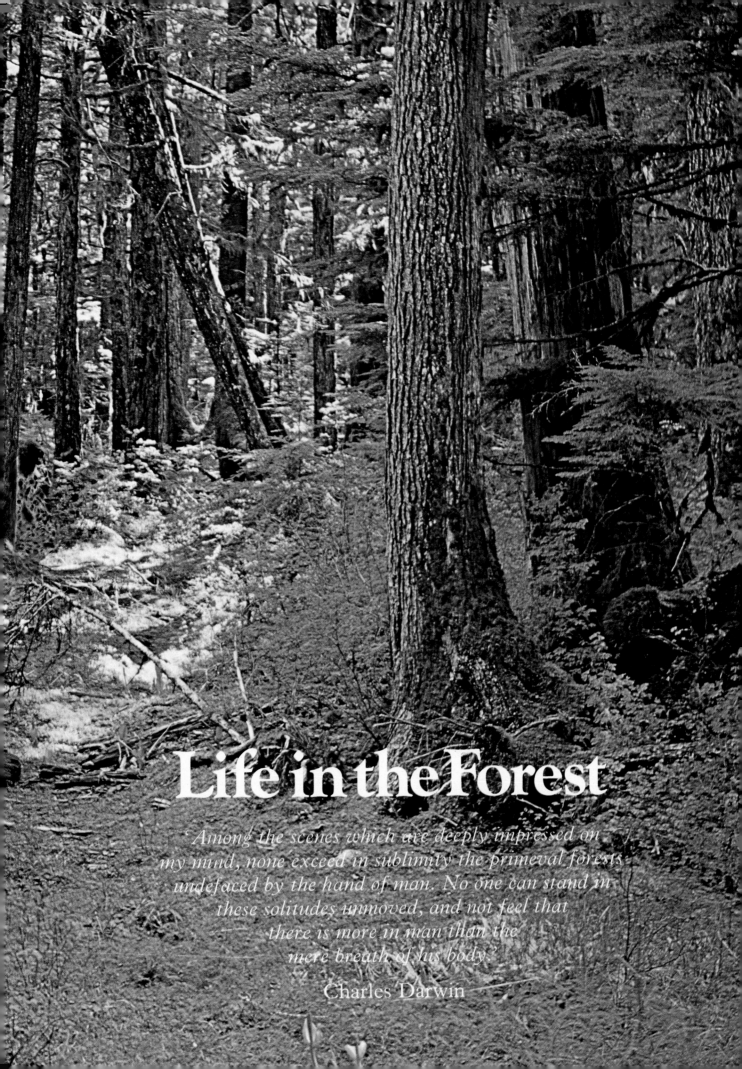

# Life in the Forest

"Among the scenes which are deeply impressed on my mind, none exceed in sublimity the primeval forests undefaced by the hand of man. No one can stand in these solitudes unmoved, and not feel that there is more in man than the mere breath of his body."

Charles Darwin

DESPITE the fact that about a third of Alaska lies above the Arctic Circle it possesses, as was mentioned earlier in this book, a very substantial amount of forest which occupies some thirty-two per cent of the total area of the state. The northern limit of tree growth is reached on the southern slopes of the Brooks Range, except that tall balsam poplars are to be found in a few favoured spots north of the mountains. Although the acreage is very substantial, the greatest proportion of forest, in central and south-central Alaska, is only of low or moderate density and is dominated by white spruce, birch, balsam poplar, willows and quaking aspen, with black spruce in wet valley-bottom habitats. True, dense forest with well developed trees is found only in the extreme south-east, in The Panhandle and on the Kenai Peninsula. In the former area the forest is dominated by Sitka spruce and western hemlock. The Seward Peninsula, the Kuskokwim-Yukon Delta area and the Alaska Peninsula are treeless. Afognak Island in the Gulf of Alaska has good forest cover, but on Kodiak Island it is more limited in extent.

There are two areas of national forest status in Alaska and the largest of these is the Tongass National Forest covering 25,000 square miles or 16,015,904 acres. It is the largest national forest in the entire United States, and the only one where the timber that is cropped has to be transported by marine waterways. The sheer rugged beauty of the Tongass area with its vistas of mist-shrouded forests, icefields, glaciers, snow-capped mountains, waterfalls and dramatic cliffs and fiords, is world famous. The wealth of wild flowers in favourable spots and the luxuriousness of the vegetation is due to the warm, humid, heavy-rainfall climate, induced by the ameliorating influence of the Japanese Current. The Chugach National Forest in south-central Alaska is the second largest in the United States and one of the first to have been withdrawn from public domain when the national forest system was created in 1891. It covers an area of 8,000 square miles or 4,726,000 acres and encompasses the islands of Prince William Sound and the adjacent mainland. The topography of the Chugach National Forest was substantially altered by the earthquake of March 1964, and it has been estimated that the resulting fault extends for something like 400 miles from the western part of Prince William Sound, south-westwards almost to Kodiak Island.

My first real acquaintance with Alaska's forests took place in May 1969 when I found myself camped with one companion in spruce forest on the north side of the Yukon River, a few miles down river from Stevens Village below the Fort Hamlin Hills. We were in fact studying not so much the forest as the spring break-up of ice on the river. This took place on 15th May and the ice went out very rapidly indeed. I found witnessing it a most attractive experience and this feeling was not completely dispelled when we discovered, on emerging one morning, that a black bear had walked through the narrow gap between the tiny one-man tents during the course of the night. On subsequent explorations through the forest in this area we found ample evidence in the form of tracks and droppings of the presence of black bears and moose. At some time in the past a considerable part of this area of forest had been burnt over, and there were the standing, gaunt skeletons of many dead spruce trees providing evidence. It was noticed that open areas had quickly been colonized by balsam poplar and birch which had formed quite dense stands. Walking through this forest one's feet sank deep into the accumulated moss and there was little to disturb the brooding silence. It is the silence of the forest by the Yukon River that sticks in my mind more than anything else on that particular trip. The silence sometimes lasted for hours, and was perhaps broken only by the

*Preceding pages* In south-east Alaska, hemlock and Sitka spruce forest reaches its peak of development as a result of the high rainfall and the absence of permafrost.

*Right* The red squirrel, whose scolding call frequently breaks the silence of the forest, is more often heard than seen.

*Below* A common inhabitant of lakes and marshes in the Alaskan interior, the muskrat constructs conical-shaped houses at the edge of water.

furious scolding of the little red squirrels (*Tamiasciurus hudsonicus*) that we sometimes disturbed. Even when we could not see or hear the squirrels, their presence was betrayed by the enormous piles of cone scales around stumps where they had been feeding. One evening at about 9.30 p.m. a great gray owl (*Strix nebulosa*) began its eerie hooting from the forest across the river from our camp, even though it was still bright and sunny.

There was one part of the forest, however, where one could be certain of seeing a fair variety of wildlife, and this was a large shallow lake in an area of muskeg on the edge of the dense forest. Here were one or two of the conical houses of the muskrat (*Ondatra zibethica*), built of peat, moss and grass and situated on the lake edge. I noticed that there were no muskrat houses on any of the handful of small islands in the lake. The animals were extremely active and not at all shy, but they went to ground whenever one of the two marsh hawks or marsh harriers (*Circus cyaneus*) that were in the vicinity passed

*Overleaf. Left* Forest gives way to mountains and soft snow blurs the outlines of the spruce trees. *Right* The black bear in Alaska is very much a forest animal. It is less aggressive than the grizzly.

overhead. I never saw a marsh hawk make any attempt to take a muskrat and would think that they would find it difficult, if not impossible, to do so. The lake was an absolute hive of activity which struck one most forcibly on emerging from the quiet of the forest. Overhead one or two common snipes (*Gallinago gallinago*) would be drumming, while out on the water were a pair of Arctic loons, mallards, shovelers, green-winged teals, pintails, buffleheads (*Bucephala albeola*), Canada geese and a pair of red-necked grebes (*Podiceps grisegena*). Very nearly all of these were indulging in courtship activities in preparation for breeding. This bubbling spirit of spring was also very evident among the various species of waders that were present. These included lesser yellowlegs (*Totanus flavipes*), long-billed dowitchers, pectoral and solitary sandpipers (*Tringa solitaria*), golden plovers and semi-palmated plovers. The solitary sandpipers and lesser yellowlegs appeared to be mated and when disturbed flew up to the top of tall spruces from where they called loudly and agitatedly. A dozen or so of the delightful tree-nesting Bonaparte's gulls (*Larus philadelphia*) were also present but did not seem yet to be paired off. Perhaps some of the ducks were simply halting for a while and would shortly continue upriver where, not so very many miles further east, lay the Yukon Flats, one of the most important waterfowl breeding areas in North America. Sometimes eighty or ninety miles wide, the 10,800 square miles of the Yukon Flats are reputed to hold some 10,000 nesting sandhill cranes (*Grus canadensis*), and a similar number of geese, and to produce at least a million young ducks each year.

As the days passed the hitherto silent forest began to show rather more signs of life. Myrtle warblers (*Dendroica coronata*) arrived and soon gave odd little snatches of song, and slate-coloured juncos (*Junco hyemalis*) began to make themselves heard. Particularly noisy were a pair or two of yellow-shafted flickers whose loud ringing notes carried a great distance. But one bird more than any other really portrayed the spirit of this vast forest, and that was the varied thrush (*Ixoreus naevius*) whose melancholy notes were sometimes heard. The coming of spring was evident in other ways too, and climbing some steep bluffs that rose above the forest on the edge of the river, we came upon dozens of enormous purple blooms of the pasqueflower (*Pulsatilla patens*). Apart from the mammals already mentioned the only other species seen here was the occasional snowshoe hare (*Lepus americanus*), but never a sign of its predator the lynx (*Lynx canadensis*). This was not surprising since in 1969 the snowshoe hare was not very evident anywhere in Alaska. Rather more were seen in 1970 and 1971 when they were common over wide areas and evidently approaching one of their population 'peaks'.

This first visit to the Yukon River country in the spring served to whet my appetite, but I did not know at that time whether or not there would be an opportunity to return there. As it happened I went back very soon afterwards when, in mid-June, I established the first of a series of temporary camps for the purpose of carrying out some preliminary ecological work along the proposed route of the trans-Alaska pipeline from the Yukon River north to Prudhoe Bay. The first camp into which my team moved was by Hess Creek a few miles upstream from its junction with the Yukon not so very far from Rampart. A southern tributary of the Yukon River, Hess Creek and its surroundings are typical of the rolling hill country of the eastern interior of Alaska. Our camp site was adjacent to several types of habitat, pure spruce forest, mixed coniferous and deciduous forest, lightly wooded dry bluffs, muskeg and riverside areas. This naturally made for a variety of wildlife. In the mud at the edge of the creek close to where

*Right* The lynx, the most important natural predator of the snowshoe hare is rarely seen in years when hares are scarce.

*Below* Despite the protective coloration of its white winter coat, this snowshoe hare remains alert to danger in the forest.

the tents were pitched were the tracks of bear, wolf and moose. The most noticeable and persistent fauna were the mosquitoes, which was hardly surprising in view of the nature of the site that we had picked for our camp.

The dense spruce forest around Hess Creek was rather livelier than had been the case two or three weeks earlier by the Yukon itself, although for much of the time a similar brooding silence prevailed, particularly on the hottest days. Underfoot was the usual deep layer of

*Overleaf* Moose River on the Kenai Peninsula winds quietly through mile after mile of spruce forest. *Inset left* In central and southern Alaska the red-necked grebe nests among the vegetation at the edge of forest lakes and pools. *Inset right* The industrious beaver is widely distributed throughout central and southern Alaska.

mosses and lichens, but remarkably few wild flowers. There was, however, the pungent odour and white flowers of Labrador tea and here and there the creamy-white blooms of large-flowered wintergreen. Once again the melancholy song of the varied thrush was heard, joined now by the nasal notes of the western wood pewee (*Contopus sordidulus*), the explosive song of ruby-crowned kinglets (*Regulus calendula*), and the raucous cries of gray jays, a pair of which were feeding their young close to our camp. The really musical performer was the fox sparrow (*Passerella iliacus*) whose one or two preliminary notes were followed by a sweet song that slid down the scale. It was curious how seldom one saw any mammals in this spruce habitat, other than the ubiquitous red squirrels that soon became bold enough to come out and run round our tents. Where the forest floor was really damp, a condition normally indicated by the presence of willow thickets, we did find a few tundra red-backed voles (*Clethrionomys rutilus*), but on the whole small rodent populations appeared to be at a very low ebb.

We could hardly miss the black bears of which I concluded there were probably six or seven different individuals in the immediate vicinity of camp. In fact I do not recall having been in any other area in Alaska where these bears were apparently so numerous. In the first couple of days in camp, before we had got properly organized, two black bears paid an early morning visit to the food cache and disposed of 200 dollars worth of meat, two dozen eggs and a large box of apples before being discovered. This was the only real trouble we had with them, other than one which made a return visit a little later and turned most aggressive when confronted.

There was one very large individual which specialized in making abrupt appearances in my vicinity. One evening while sitting quietly by the creek watching a beaver (*Castor canadensis*) that had made its appearance, I heard a slight noise and looked up to see this bear coming along a well worn track which passed some twenty-five feet or so from where I was sitting. Sensing (and hoping) that I had not been seen I remained motionless and the bear walked by snuffling and snorting, but I was a little disconcerted when he was immediately followed by a second bear. On another occasion I was again by the creek, this time watching a pair of belted kingfishers (*Megaceryle alcyon*), when a movement on the opposite bank attracted my attention and I looked across to find a sow with her two year old cub watching me with great interest. This may have been the same sow that next day gave me a nasty shock. On this occasion, armed with nothing more lethal than a pond net, I was standing at the edge of a pool adjacent to a large stand of spruce trying to catch some of the numerous dragonflies that were flying about, when a black bear cub started from the undergrowth ahead and then sat down and looked at me. Realizing that the sow must be nearby I turned to beat a retreat in the opposite direction, only to find her standing motionless right in my path. Keeping a wary eye on both sow and offspring, and sweating profusely, I paced slowly backwards in the only direction left open and eventually gained the shelter of the trees. Had it been a grizzly rather than a black bear, I doubt if I would have got off so lightly.

The contrast between the shade of the dense spruce forest and the sunlit slopes of the dry bluffs that rose above the creek was most marked. On these bluffs were a few scattered white spruce, but mostly the trees were quaking aspens and balsam poplars, tall slender trees with pale bark and beautiful light green leaves through which the sun slanted to form a dappled pattern on the ground below. Here was an ideal observation post, since one could look across the forest and away over the creeks and muskeg beyond, and, best of all, there were hardly any mosquitoes. There were remarkably few flowers out on these dry bluffs at the time, but a violet-coloured species of beard-tongue (*Penstemon gormani*), a member of the figwort family, was quite noticeable. Gazing down upon the spruce forest canopy one became aware of just a little more activity than was evident when walking on the forest floor. A pair of Arctic warblers moved slowly about the tops of some tall spruces immediately below where I was sitting. They did not utter a sound, which was in direct contrast to the excited calls of the many redpolls that rose above the trees in constant excited flight. A few pairs of soberly coloured but remarkably beautiful bohemian waxwings (*Bombycilla garrula*) could be seen hawking for insects from vantage points on the taller trees. The really intense activity was provided by the graceful violet-green swallows (*Tachycineta thalassina*) that flashed back and forth with rapid, darting flight, feeding on the myriad insects that danced in clouds above the forest. As the birds twisted and turned the brilliant sun struck metallic reflections of green and purple, like shot silk, from their plumage. High above in the great blue dome of the sky, a pair of red-tailed hawks (*Buteo jamaicensis*) soared in wide circles.

As any ecologist knows, it is usually the forest edge where the greatest variety of life is found, particularly if there is also water, and this area was no exception. With the temperature standing at some 80°F perhaps more birds than usual were attracted to the vicinity of the water. We were actually camped by an isolated and partly dried out oxbow off the main creek, and the damp area between the water and the dense forest was covered with thickets of willow, alder and quaking aspen, enlivened by the yellow blooms of shrubby cinquefoil (*Potentilla fruticosa*). Many of these trees reached a good height, perhaps because permafrost was absent from the immediate vicinity of the creek. Except during the hottest part of the day, there were always many birds singing from within the thickets – robin, yellow warbler (*Dendroica petechia*), orange-crowned warbler (*Vermivora celata*), Wilson's warbler (*Wilsonia pusilla*) and northern waterthrush (*Seiurus noveboracensis*). One only actually saw these warblers on odd occasions and then only at the cost of much patience, but other birds were more in evidence. Swainson's thrushes (*Hylocichla ustulata*), for instance, made periodic 'flycatching' flights from the willows, flying low over the water on a course that was generally parallel with the adjacent trees. High up in the taller trees the little Traill's flycatcher (*Empidonax traillii*) remained inactive for long periods, occasionally uttering its characteristic sneezy song and making the odd flight after passing insects. Rusty blackbirds (*Euphagus carolinus*) were constantly feeding among the horsetails (*Equisetum* species) and other marsh plants, often wading up to their bellies in the water. I never saw them take any interest in the brilliant swallowtail butterflies that frequently settled on the damp mud. Waders are not normally regarded as forest birds, but the solitary sandpiper has some claim in that respect, since it nests in trees. Several individuals were present in the vicinity of our camp and eventually one was discovered sitting on four eggs in a ridiculously small nest about fifteen feet up in a black spruce. Small, with a shallow cup, this was probably the old nest of a Traill's flycatcher.

From the forested interior of Alaska, a small part of which I have attempted to describe, one travels south across the mighty Alaska Range and the Chugach Mountains to the Gulf of Alaska, the area where Alaska's forests reach the peak of development, and now we shall look briefly at the forests of the Kenai Peninsula and The Panhandle.

Some two-thirds of the Kenai Peninsula in the west are occupied by lowlands which are a mosaic of rolling hills, muskeg, forests of quaking

*Above* Devil's club is a densely prickly shrub which often forms nearly impenetrable thickets in the moist woods of southern and south-east Alaska.

*Right* As fall comes to the Kenai Peninsula the leaves of the aspens turn orange and gold to provide a sea of brilliant colour.

*Opposite* A female Sitka black-tailed deer steps quietly along a forest stream.

aspen, willow, birch and spruce, dotted with about 1,200 lakes and not
far short of 200 miles of streams and rivers. There are two very large
glacial lakes, Lake Tustumena of 73,000 acres and Skilak of 24,000
acres. The remaining one-third of the peninsula is occupied by the
majestic Kenai Mountains. It is here on Kenai Peninsula that the 2,700
square mile (1,730,000 acre) Kenai National Moose Range was established in 1941, and which today is inhabited by between 7,000 and
8,000 giant moose for which Kenai has long been world famous. This is
a habitat that they share with the black bear, the beaver, the mink
(*Mustela vison*) and the elusive lynx, for instance. Proposals have been
made to include 1,040,000 acres of the Kenai National Moose Range in
the national wilderness preservation system.

My best memories of Kenai are related to leisurely canoe trips across
numerous lakes and along winding rivers where one passes beaver
lodges and dams, cow moose and their calves browsing on the succulent
aquatic vegetation or a hawk owl (*Surnia ulula*) atop a spruce. One of
the great advantages of canoe travel through forest waterways is its
silence. That this sometimes has its drawbacks we found one day on the
Moose River when, drifting quietly round a loop in the river, we
found ourselves only yards from a cow moose and her calf which were
feeding in mid-river. The calf was for a while unable to find a spot
where it could clamber up the bank and the cow, her maternal instincts
aroused, began to charge the canoe but at the last minute, and to our
great relief, decided that she should go and help her calf get ashore.
Instead of paddling quietly round the perimeter of the lakes, some
travellers hurry across in a direct line from one portage to the next. In
doing so they may well miss much of the wealth of waterfowl that
frequent the lakes, such as the common loons or great northern divers
(*Gavia immer*), red-necked grebes, surf scoters (*Melanitta perspicillata*),
goldeneyes (*Bucephala clangula*), wigeons, shovelers, pintails, green-
winged teals and the delicate Bonaparte's gulls whose nests will be
found in trees near the water. Worse still they may miss the chance of
seeing the rarest of North America's swans, the trumpeter swan (*Olor
buccinator*) which has a flourishing breeding population on the Kenai
Peninsula, where a 1968 census revealed the presence of just over 180
adults and cygnets.

I remember also the pleasure of beaching the canoe and setting up
camp at the forest edge. Beneath the trees is the usual deep layer of
mosses and lichens, perhaps enlivened by the blooms of ground dog-
wood (*Cornus canadensis*), baneberry (*Actaea rubra*), blueberry
(*Vaccinium alaskensis*) and lingonberry (*V. vitis-idaea*). The latter is most
attractive with its pink flowers in small nodding clusters. Nature not
only provides this aesthetically pleasing setting, she also provides background music in the form of the songs of birds such as the redpoll,
white-crowned sparrow (*Zonotricha leucophrys*), myrtle warbler, black-
poll warbler (*Dendroica striata*) and the gray-cheeked thrush (*Hylocichla
minima*), while echoing from lake to lake are the mournful wails of the
common loon and the trumpet-like call of the trumpeter swan.
Companionship comes also in the form of red squirrels, bold gray jays
or camp robbers, and the inquisitive scolding figures of black-capped
chickadees (*Parus atricapillus*) and boreal chickadees (*P. hudsonicus*). It
must have been experiences such as this that inspired George Shiras III
to write of his 1911 Kenai journeys, 'Were all of Alaska erased from the
map except Kenai Peninsula and its immediately adjacent waters, there
would yet remain in duplicate that which constitutes the more unique
and that which typifies the whole of this wonderful country.' There is a
point about the gray-cheeked thrush that is worth mentioning, since I
noticed it here on the Kenai Peninsula and also in the vicinity of the

A common loon or great northern diver, sleek and streamlined
in build, sits tightly on its nest by
a lake in the Alaskan interior.

Kanuti River north of the Yukon. This is the apparent preference of this species for areas of forest that have been burnt by forest fires within about the preceding twenty years, and also their tendency to occur in pockets forming what might almost be called loose colonies.

Finally there is the incredible Panhandle, where both forest and towns such as Ketchikan, Wrangell and Juneau, are squeezed into a narrow belt between sea and mountains. Generally speaking the forest extends up to about 2,500 to 3,000 feet, with the mountain hemlock replacing the western hemlock at the higher altitudes. Here we are in the highest rainfall areas of Alaska where a mean annual precipitation of 200 inches or more is normal, and where the number of days in the year on which rain does not fall are minimal. As a result these coastal forests are permanently dripping wet, the trees may reach a height of 300 feet and they are draped with epiphytic mosses. On the floor of the forest it is dark and wet and wild flowers are scarce or may be absent altogether. However, here we can find some species that can be regarded as characteristic of this specialized humid habitat. There is the calypso orchid or fairy slipper (*Calypso bulbosa*), for instance, with its broad purple-spotted lip, and the red coral-root orchid (*Corallorhiza maculata*) which in Alaska is confined to The Panhandle, as is the saprophytic Indian pipe (*Monotropa hypopitys*). The copper flower (*Cladothamnus pyrolaeflorus*), single-flowered wintergreen (*Moneses uniflora*), twin-flower (*Linnaea borealis*) and yellow skunk cabbage (*Lysichiton americanum*) will also be encountered, together with two unpleasant shrubs, the devil's club (*Echinopanax horridum*) and rusty menziesia (*Menziesia ferruginea*) with its disagreeable odour. From late April until August, the tiny rufous hummingbird (*Selasphorus rufus*) that has come all the way from its winter home in Central America will feed and rest in this rain-soaked corner of Alaska. To see this brilliant little bird hovering on invisible wings before a flower in the pouring rain is a really fascinating sight. The hummingbird does in fact reach as far north as the Yukon area, but the same cannot be said of the handsome Steller's jay (*Cyanocitta stelleri*) which can only be found in the forests as far north as Kenai and Seward. This jay can be a source of irritation to the naturalist as I found in the forest above Seward one day, for it will often fly ahead calling loudly, and thus alerting any animal in the vicinity.

These rain-soaked coastal forests of south-east Alaska are the natural habitat of the Sitka black-tailed deer (*Odocoileus hemionus*), whose population is estimated at around the quarter of a million level. In summer they leave the forests to range over the high alpine areas. During periods of deep snow these little deer become almost shore animals, frequenting a narrow zone adjacent to the beaches. Here, too, bald eagles (*Haliaeetus leucocephalus*) will gather to feed on those that die.

This, then, has been a brief journey through a tiny portion of Alaska's vast forest regions, from stunted spruces by the Yukon River to towering hemlocks and cedar in the south-east. Every type has something to offer, be it spruce in the bottomlands, birch and balsam poplars on the mountain slopes, or dripping hemlocks in the rainforest. To appreciate the sheer beauty of the forests, however, it is necessary to wait until the fall, in September and October. Then, wherever there is quaking aspen, birch or poplar, and before the first frosts and the soft blanket of winter snow, there will be a few weeks of unbelievable colour, with red, gold, yellow and russet, scattered in profusion among the evergreen of the conifers. Slashes of brilliant colour spread across one of nature's vast canvasses with a backdrop of brooding mountains on which the first fresh white snow of winter has already fallen. This is Alaska in one of her most beautiful moods.

# The Alaska Range and the Chugach Mountains

*'Tis distance lends enchantment to the view,*
*And robes the mountain in its azure hue.*

Thomas Campbell

ALTHOUGH the Alaska Range includes among its peaks the highest mountain in North America, Mount McKinley, it is not in fact a very lofty range, the crest only averaging between 7,000 and 9,000 feet in altitude. Its impressiveness lies in the large number of icefields and glaciers that it contains and in the accentuated loftiness of the few high peaks that abut directly on to the neighbouring lowlands, such as the great wall which faces the Tanana–Kuskokwim lowlands. As one can see on looking at a physical map, this range really consists of four great mountain massifs, which are snow- and ice-covered even at the height of summer, and some of which are usually visible from Anchorage as a white wall on the distant horizon. It is a relatively narrow range, being only some thirty miles in width near the Canadian border, increasing to sixty miles around Mount McKinley, and finally to twice that in the vicinity of Mount Spurr, which lies almost due west of Anchorage as the range bends southwards from the area of Mount McKinley. On the 9th July 1953 Mount Spurr spewed out a thirteen mile high mushroom of ash and steam.

These four fairly discrete mountain groups comprising the Alaska Range are breached by several rivers and a few low passes. Two of these routes through the range are accessible by road from Anchorage; the Glenn Highway from Gakona to Tok running through the Mentasta Pass in the east, and the Richardson Highway following the valley of the Delta River. In this valley are two points of more than passing interest. The first, near Rapids, is the Black Rapids Glacier which has its beginnings in the high peaks around Mount Hayes and descends to the Delta Valley. In the winter of 1936 to 1937 this glacier advanced no less than four miles in six months and came to within half a mile of the highway. Oddly enough this rapid advance was followed by an equally rapid retreat. Further north, near Delta Junction, one stands the chance of seeing the herd of 350 to 400 bison (*Bison bison*) which inhabit the district. In summer they range south and west along the Delta River valley to the mountains, while in winter they concentrate in the general vicinity of Clearwater Lake. I have seen this herd in the Delta Valley in the summer months, but despite their great size they somehow do not seem very impressive. Perhaps when they thundered in their thousands across the plains of the west it was a different story. Fine views of the southern aspects of Mount Deborah, Hess Mountain and Mount Hayes can be obtained from the Denali Highway between Paxson and Cantwell. From this quarter they are seen as a group of spire-like mountains with icefields and glaciers. One of these, the Susitna Glacier, exhibits some quite striking deformed morainal ridges, probably a result of powerful ice surges from tributary streams. Away to the west, clouds permitting, the great bulk of Mount McKinley and its neighbours will be seen.

Tremendous views of the Alaska Range are obtained when flying the commercial route from Anchorage to Fairbanks, and in particular there are panoramic views of the Eldridge and Muldrow Glaciers and the landscape that they have sculptured as they wind down from the Mount McKinley group. In the winter of 1956 to 1957, the Muldrow Glacier underwent a sudden rapid surge of movement, which was accompanied by a pronounced lowering of the ice level in the higher reaches. The recent opening of a new super highway from Anchorage to McKinley and Fairbanks means that the Mount McKinley National Park is now an easy drive from Anchorage. Formerly it could only be reached by road by taking the long way round along the Glenn and Richardson Highways to Paxson, and then along the famous unsurfaced Denali Highway, a drive that could be quite an adventure in itself. The new highway means, inevitably, a great increase in the numbers of people

*Preceding pages* Willows come into leaf soon after the snow melts on the high tundra of the Alaska Range.

visiting Mount McKinley National Park with its one road through to Wonder Lake. This is bound to create problems and will have an effect on animal life in the immediate vicinity of the park road. Quite possibly it may be that in future years only those who are able and willing to back-pack away from the road and into the mountains will see the best of the wildlife.

Along the southern flank of the Alaska Range the mountains soar impressively above the Susitna Valley, but are separated from the higher peaks of the range by a belt of lower mountains and foothills. Naturally enough the topmost ridges and peaks are barren and inhospitable and many are snow-covered at all times. Nevertheless this range of mountains has a fine alpine flora. Up above 6,600 feet, apart from lichens, the flora is far from rich but this is compensated for by the beauty of colour and form. In the dry alpine heaths we shall certainly find the mountain avens, the Arctic poppy, the tiny alpine azalea (*Loiseleuria procumbens*) which will tolerate quite acidic conditions, and the white bell-shaped flowers of the evergreen Lapland cassiope or mountain heather (*Cassiope tetragona*). On ridges and sandy substrata the moss campion is present, while scree slopes and ledges will support roseroot (*Sedum rosea*). Among damp rocks and on solifluction soils the purple mountain saxifrage is a characteristic species. We may also find, where there are dry heath conditions, the Alaska moss heath (*Cassiope stellariana*), although this is more common in the Chugach and other coastal mountains. On gravelly and rock sites the creamy-flowered diapensia (*Diapensia lapponica*) occurs up to an altitude of about 4,900 feet, but the bearberry whose leaves provide such a splash of red in the fall does not grow much above 3,300 feet.

The majority of these high alpine flowers are not, of course, by any means confined to the Alaska Range, but occur also in the Brooks Range and in the coastal mountains round the Gulf of Alaska. Scree slopes and gravelly areas up to about 6,600 feet are also the habitat for alpine hawksbeard and the beautiful pink Scammon's spring beauty (*Claytonia scammaniana*) which is confined to the Alaska Range. The latter species is also associated with snow beds up to a similar altitude, where it may also be accompanied by the pink Alaskan spring beauty (*Claytonia sarmentosa*) which, unlike Scammon's spring beauty, extends north into the Brooks Range, and also the northern windflower (which grows right down to the forest edge), Lessing's arnica (*Arnica lessingii*) and the snow cinquefoil (*Potentilla hyparctica*).

While it is the delicate alpine flowers and the superb views that make walking the high tops so exhilarating, there are other forms of life too. I well remember my first encounter at 9 p.m. on a June evening with the smallest and rarest of Alaska's three species of ptarmigan, the white-tailed ptarmigan (*Lagopus leucurus*). In summer this bird lives right up to the edge of the permanent snow and icefields, that is to say it is often found at even higher elevations than the rock ptarmigan. Despite its exposed habitat the white-tailed ptarmigan is difficult to see, since it blends into the background in a remarkable way. Its presence is often first revealed by its peculiar call which consists of a three-syllabled high-pitched scream. Other birds that can be found at these high levels are the water pipit (*Anthus spinoletta*), the horned lark and the attractive gray-crowned rosy finch (*Leucosticte tephronotis*), not to mention the magnificent golden eagle. This bird of prey feeds very heavily on the Arctic ground squirrel in the Alaska Range, as does also the gyrfalcon.

The tree line of white spruce in the Alaska Range extends upwards to as much as 3,500 feet in places and is often bordered at its upper edge by an all but impenetrable belt of mountain alder which is characterized

*Left* The yellow and gold of birch and aspen contrast with the green of spruce as fall comes to the forests of the Chugach Mountains.

*Below* August in central Alaska. Fireweed brings a splash of colour, which is heightened by the lowering storm clouds over the mountains.

*Right* Winter grips the land and Mount Susitna is seen through frost-covered trees.

by a markedly horizontal growth. A bird which one is almost certain to encounter in this habitat is the golden-crowned sparrow (*Zonotrichia atricapilla*) whose wistful song is accurately rendered as 'I-seeee-you' on a descending note. As one descends from the alpine to the sub-alpine environment changes in the flora become evident. On the southern slopes of the Alaska Range the sub-alpine meadows have a flora which includes a few species whose main distribution is decidedly oceanic, notably the northern cranesbill (*Geranium erianthum*), swertia (*Swertia perennis*) and, much less commonly, the Kamchatka fritillary (*Fritillaria camschatcensis*) or black lily as it is sometimes called. The latter is found much more frequently in the montane meadows of the Chugach Mountains and the St Elias Range. Species with a much wider distribution that are found in these sub-alpine meadows are the white camass (*Zygadenus elegans*) which may persist up to 6,600 feet and therefore qualifies as an alpine species, monkshood (*Aconitum delphinifolium*) which may extend up to the 5,600 foot contour, and the Arctic lupine

94

Unconvinced that there is any danger, a hoary marmot looks curiously at the photographer.

and the forget-me-not (*Myosotis alpestris*) both of which normally die out around 4,900 feet. The damper meadows, in addition to the species already mentioned, commonly also have larkspur (*Delphinium glaucum*) and Jacob's ladder. On gazing across these high meadows one notices immediately that the colours of the most numerous flowers are predominantly blue or purple. Seen from a distance such meadows appear as a blue haze on the mountain slopes.

One of the common mammals of the Alaska Range is the hoary marmot (*Marmota caligata*) which can be found up to quite high altitudes. It occurs also in the Brooks Range where I have seen them up to 4,000 feet or so, but in the Alaska Range I have seen them at 4,600 feet, although at that elevation they were not common. It would be interesting to know the maximum altitude at which these animals occur in the Brooks and Alaska Ranges. The hoary marmot always looks fat. It passes the winter in a state of hibernation in a den deep in the rocks where it is unaffected by the prolonged cold and deep snow, which it dislikes. During this period it draws on its fat reserves and awakes at intervals to urinate and dispose of metabolic wastes. In late summer it collects quantities of dry grass which is taken into the den for the winter nest. However, I have also watched this grass collecting in late May, when the nest was most likely being prepared for the birth of the young.

Marmots seem to live in loose colonies in suitable habitat and extensive intervening areas are often quite devoid of them. The types of habitat in which to seek hoary marmots include steep canyon sides, large isolated rock outcrops, scree slopes with large rocks and jumbles of boulders at the foot of talus slopes. With its colour pattern of grey, shading off to cinnamon towards the hips and often deep russet-brown on the tail, the marmot is sometimes difficult to see despite its fair bulk. This is particularly so when they are motionless against a background of rocks with crustose lichens. Being herbivores, the marmots often graze on well vegetated slopes at a distance from their dens, sometimes in close proximity to Dall sheep. But the dens are almost invariably located on steep rock slopes and similar sites where a grizzly would have great difficulty in digging them out.

The presence of marmots is frequently first revealed by their penetrating shrill alarm whistle which, when uttered in narrow canyons, echoes round the walls to some effect. It will be found that there are always observation points in strategic positions in the vicinity of the dens overlooking regularly used grazing areas. One thing that intrigues me is the fact that these marmots become particularly alarmed at the appearance of a golden eagle and when one appears whistles sound in all directions as the alarm is passed on. This implies that the golden eagle is a predator of these animals, and yet I have never seen an eagle attempt to take one and have found no marmot remains at any of the four eagle eyries that I have examined, although Arctic ground squirrel corpses were always present.

I find watching hoary marmots a really fascinating experience. Fat and contented in appearance, they can be seen on warm sunny days sprawled out on rocks in postures of idle abandon. Sometimes they will choose a rock with a narrow flattish ridge and then lie with all four legs hanging over the edge, for all the world like a fur rug draped out to air. Even on these occasions they are watchful, and I remember watching half a dozen or so sunning themselves on a rock outcrop on a hot afternoon. Suddenly two alarm whistles rang out and every marmot instantaneously rushed for its den and a moment later a rough-legged hawk closely pursued by a gyrfalcon flashed overhead.

When grazing, hoary marmots stuff the succulent vegetation into their mouths at a rapid rate, occasionally stopping for a look round.

There can be few more charming sights than marmots grazing on a grassy slope carpeted with the white flowers of mountain avens and the bright yellow of one of the rock roses (*Potentilla* species), but there are many spots in the Alaska Range where this is possible. Hoary marmots are also very playful, and I have often seen one that is grazing suddenly stop, run across to another individual and indulge in a brief bout of wrestling. If this takes place on a steep slope the two animals may roll for some distance in a close embrace. Other forms of behaviour include stand-up sparring matches, gentle face-to-face nibbling and fast chases that may involve several individuals. The interesting thing about these forms of behaviour is that they are best described as, for want of a better term, 'play fighting', for they commence quite spontaneously and appear to be perfectly innocuous in character. In fact I do not remember seeing any real aggressiveness between marmots.

The average tourist to Alaska, and for that matter many resident Alaskans, are likely to gain most of their experience of the Alaska Range by visiting the Mount McKinley National Park. Covering an area of 3,030 square miles of mountains, glaciers, lakes, rivers tundra, muskeg and forest, this park affords access to a typical variety of Alaska Range habitats and their associated flora and fauna. The one road which runs from the Nenana River at the park entrance through to Wonder Lake more or less parallels the mountains, and for the majority of its route cuts through the 5,000 foot high northern foothills, passing through forest and tundra, and finally, for the last twenty miles or so, crosses an old pond-studded glacial moraine. Not many will aspire to climb to the top of mighty Mount McKinley, which dominates the entire area, its north face rising sheer for about 15,000 feet from a base plain that is itself 3,000 feet above sea level. If they did they would be able to gaze in awe at the 100,000 square mile view which led Bradford Washburn, one of the first men to reach the summit of this mountain, to write that it was 'like looking out of the very windows of heaven'. Centuries ago the Indians named this mountain Denali, meaning the Great One.

The attractions of the Mount McKinley area are extremely varied, every corner rounded opens up new vistas and brings fresh surprises. Scenes looked at time and time again never pall and always appear different, not only from season to season but even from hour to hour as cloud, sun and shadows impose their mood on the landscape. An enormous amount can be seen from the road, but the real wilderness enthusiast will not rest content with this. To enjoy the greatest delights and the real intimate atmosphere of this area one should aim to cross the next ridge, for it is those who shoulder a back-pack and tramp into the hinterland who will benefit the most. There are virtually no marked trails in McKinley country for there is no real need for them. One can penetrate miles into the mountains along the braided beds of the numerous rivers, or by following high ridges and crossing the open tundra. The Toklat River can be followed north along the base of the Wyoming Hills to the forested flats beyond where huge bull moose disappear into thickets without the snapping of a twig. Alternatively one can go upriver towards the glaciers and icefields in the high peaks around Mount Pendleton, or try the valleys of the Sanctuary or Savage Rivers. All are rewarding and bring their own thrills and excitements, among which are the grizzlies, for this is first class bear country.

Growing on the gravel bars are flowers that we encountered in the same habitat on the Arctic Slope, river beauty and Eskimo potato for instance, but there is also a new species that can hardly be missed. This is the Eskimo rhubarb (*Polygonum alaskanum*), a tall plant with a mass of yellowish white flowers. It is found throughout central Alaska.

*Above* In the Alaska Range, tall spire-like spruces are reflected in the still waters of a lake.

*Opposite above* The northern cranesbill has an oceanic distribution in southern Alaska.

*Opposite below* A hoary marmot pauses from grazing on the rich flora of an alpine pasture.

While bears are not difficult to observe here the same cannot be said of the wolf, although the wolves of McKinley have been famous for years. Despite the fact that several packs are present in Mount McKinley National Park I have not seen them, but I have seen a number of individuals and sometimes two or three together. Certainly the most exciting incident involving the wolf was that which occurred in mid-June 1971.

It had been one of those glorious days, brilliantly sunny with white cottonwool clouds scudding across a blue sky. Up near Wonder Lake where summer was late in coming, greater scaups, horned or slavonian grebes (*Podiceps auritus*) and oldsquaws in full breeding plumage swam excitedly on the morainal pools; a superb male marsh hawk had been seen quartering a marshy area; and on the high tundra wheatears and water pipits were seen flitting around. There were caribou on the move along the valleys and we had seen one group of about 600 or so, composed entirely of cows, calves and yearlings. Early in the evening as we descended towards the improbably coloured scenery of Polychrome Pass, a mass of caribou were spotted in the valley below. Spread out over the valley floor in scattered groups they were moving slowly eastwards. Suddenly a ripple of movement was evident among the animals nearest to us, and a lone black wolf was seen moving in from the cover of some low scrub.

The wolf broke into a run as alarm spread through the nearest groups of caribou. Soon it became clear that he had singled out a young calf, and passing many other individuals in the now running herd he closed in for the kill, increasing speed as the distance closed. Here was real poetry of movement, the lithe form of the black wolf flowing powerfully over the ground, and the caribou at full gallop. The wolf took the calf with a leap from the side, stood by it for a few moments and then ran off a short distance to gaze after the now scattered herd. At this moment the downed calf got to its feet and ran off again. A short chase and it was down for the second time. The wolf was lying still as another group of caribou, apparently unaware of what had been happening ahead of them, began to pass close by. The wolf leapt up and after another short sharp chase brought down a second calf and I was able to see through field glasses that this one was killed outright. Leaving the two kills the wolf wandered off along the valley and some time later commenced pursuing a bunch of adult, cow caribou, but abandoned this when it was clear that he was being outrun. For some fifteen minutes the wolf lay in the shelter of some small bushes, and then started after a further group of passing cows but was again outpaced. Eventually, ignoring the two kills he had made, the wolf wandered off towards the hills, perhaps with the intention of coming back with other members of his group. As he departed a raven and a golden eagle were already at work on one of the kills, and the rest of the caribou were peacefully grazing as though nothing had happened.

That incredible slice of luck, of being in the right place at just the right moment and seeing a wolf go through the whole process of stalking, selecting, pursuing and killing its prey, is not the sort of thing that happens very often, in fact perhaps only once in a lifetime. Oddly enough another wolf incident, this time involving a whitish wolf, had occurred in July of the previous summer, on the wide floor of Thorofare Pass. The white wolf, accompanied by four other light-coloured individuals who may have been young of the year before, killed and fed on a caribou. Some time later, while the group of five were resting a short distance from the carcass, a black wolf appeared and gorged on the remains without interference. As he made off, however, he was pursued for a long way by the white wolves which appeared to attack him and leave him dead. On examination it was found that there were no external injuries on this black wolf, but the stomach was so full that the animal had tried to disgorge while running and had evidently choked to death.

Looking back over the notes of my wanderings in the Mount McKinley area, innumerable events come to life again. One particular incident is as vivid now as it was at the time it occurred in early September 1969. It was a little after noon and we were out on the tundra about three miles south-east of Wonder Lake. Suddenly the air was filled with clarion music from an unseen source, and eventually some 1,000 sandhill cranes in six great V formations passed over very high up and heading south. A quarter of an hour or so later the noise increased in volume and more cranes appeared from the north flying on a broad front, mostly in V formations but some in long straggling lines. All were heading south and when approximately in our vicinity the various groups coalesced and began to spiral, in a great circling mass, in order to gain height. Their approach from the north was at about 8,000 feet, and on breaking off at the top of the spiral they were at something like twice that altitude. Some groups, in fact, were passing over the top of Mount McKinley. Altogether some 5,000 cranes passed over in thirty minutes, surely one of nature's great sights.

I also recall a warm June day along the Savage River when, as I was passing a rock slide, my attention was attracted by a curious sharp and rather nasal 'yonk'. Just the one call, then silence. It was a good fifteen minutes before a sudden movement caught my eye and there on a rock was a little collared pika (*Ochotona collaris*) and a call from higher up indicated the presence of another. I watched this small relative of the rabbit (it is sometimes called the rock rabbit) for about an hour and was fascinated by the quantity of grass and leaves that it carried down into three or four separate cavities. This is how the pika ensures its winter food supply, literally by making hay. I have found other collared pika colonies in these mountains, for example along the East Fork of the Toklat River and in Polychrome Pass, but never have I found pikas and hoary marmots occupying the same spots. Clearly there is a difference in habitat selection, although there may well be places where they occur together.

Then there was another June day, spent travelling down the Savage River, when it was warm and sunny and the mosquitoes became a bit of a nuisance, but the banks were a mass of flowers including such colourful gems as the Arctic poppy, the alpine shooting star and the few-flowered cordyalis (*Cordyalis pauciflora*) with its small purplish-blue drooping flowers. As we entered the narrow canyon at the foot of Mount Margaret a flock of nine Dall sheep, all ewes, which were grazing on the slope beyond the river, lifted their heads only briefly. Once through the canyon there was a view across the wooded flats to the next line of hills, but we turned west along the southern slopes of Mount Margaret, passing through dwarf birch, willows and alder where redpolls and white-crowned sparrows sang. Reaching Pinto Creek we turned south and began the long steep climb up to what is locally known as Primrose Ridge, lying at over 4,000 feet, between Mount Wright and Mount Margaret. As we ascended beyond the scrub hoary marmots whistled in alarm from high rocks and a bunch of eleven Dall sheep, all rams this time, ran across a steep scree slope and over a far ridge, pausing for a moment on the skyline to look back at us. On top of the ridge it was cold, bare and windswept, but here was a little jewel of a flower. The wedge-leaved primrose (*Primula cuneifolia*) was barely an inch in height with small deep rose-pink petals. We felt that all the effort had been worthwhile.

Dall sheep are interesting animals to study particularly when they have small lambs. One such group that I watched consisted of four yearlings and a mature ewe with a tiny lamb. It was clear that the adult ewe was the leader of the group, for when two of the younger animals began to spar head to head they were soon butted apart by her. When the band was resting the lamb was in constant motion, running from one to another and leaping back and forth over their backs. One could hardly imagine a more charming sight. These sheep are uneasy when crossing valley floors between mountains, and some rivers are formidable obstacles in June when they are high with melt-water. A flock of two mature and seven younger ewes that I saw at the side of Igloo Creek, below Cathedral Mountain, were clearly unhappy at the prospect of crossing the water. One of the adults jumped in and was immediately washed downriver but managed to regain the bank. After ten minutes hesitation and several false starts she tried again, got across, and was hesitantly followed one by one by the rest of the group.

When all is said and done it is the bears that are the monarchs of the mountains, tundra and forest of the Alaska Range, and they provide that element of danger which is the real spice of life when back-packing in the wilderness. The grizzly found in the McKinley area is sometimes known as the Toklat grizzly because the core of its range is the Toklat River area. It is characterized by being very blond, shading to dark

*Above* Ross' avens, an attractive yellow species of the rose family.

*Above centre* A grizzly bear, hackles rising on its hump, eyes the photographer across the carcass of a moose that it has covered with debris.

*Right* Icebergs on the 600 foot deep lake of Portage Glacier in the Chugach Mountains.

*Above* A collared pika in the Alaska Range. This small rock-dwelling mammal is a close relative of the snowshoe hare.

*Left* An October scene in the Chugach Mountains near Valdez, southern Alaska.

brown on the underside of the body and on the legs. My first
encounter with one of these grizzlies was another amazing piece of luck
at the beginning of September 1969. We found one on a moose kill, the
partly consumed body being covered with a mass of debris that the
bear had raked together. When sighted the bear was gnawing at the
hindquarters and in the course of the next hour I managed to get to
within fifty feet and take a series of photographs. At that distance the
bear was beginning to lose patience and the hackles on its hump rose
up, but it contented itself with menacing glares. This sort of behaviour
with grizzlies is not to be recommended, but I had no intention of
passing by such a rare opportunity. I was interested to see that four
black-billed magpies were hanging around and on every opportunity
they would nip in for a titbit. This irritated the bear, who several times
swiped at the birds.

Sows with cubs are always worth watching, and late in May near
Sable Pass I came upon one with a year-old cub. Both were engaged in
digging for roots, but the youngster used far too much effort and had
to sit on his haunches from time to time for a rest. In 1971 I saw a sow
with two cubs of the year, one very blond and the other dark brown.
They were feeding on an extensive grassy area by the Toklat River,
near Divide Mountain, and the sow was so alert that our movements a
quarter of a mile away caused her to look steadily in our direction. As
the wind was not in our favour she must also have scented us. Then
there is the funny side of bear behaviour, like that of the large dark
brown individual who, wandering across a hillside, came to a small
hollow. Turning round he settled into this as though it were an arm-
chair and proceeded to slowly scratch his belly with an air of great
enjoyment. I also remember a small blond bear that had gone to sleep
on a snow patch, lying on his belly with all four legs splayed out and
nose pushed into the snow. The reaction of other animals to bears is
also amusing on occasions. I witnessed, for example, a large bull moose
browsing on some willow bushes and stopping periodically to peer
over them at a bear digging for roots in the river bed hardly a hundred
feet away. Again there are sights that remain indelibly imprinted on the
mind. One such was that of two mature Toklat grizzlies stalking
majestically along a 3,000 foot ridge near Sable Mountain, sharply
outlined against a blue sky.

Mount McKinley National Park can always produce a surprise, but
perhaps one of the strangest must be the sight of a red fox and a
wolverine (*Gulo luscus*) that came trotting side by side through scrub by
Jenny Creek. The wolverine, with its reputation for viciousness and bad
temper, is not noted for being sociable!

The general character and location of the Chugach Mountains was
outlined earlier. Much of this range is as rugged and wild as the Alaska
Range and is as full of icefields and glaciers. Nevertheless, because of
the Seward, Glenn and Richardson Highways, large parts of these
mountains are readily reached from Anchorage. One of the most
accessible glaciers in Alaska is Portage Glacier, which can be reached via
the Seward Highway from Anchorage. The change in temperature (and
often also the weather) as one leaves the main road and penetrates the
valley is often quite dramatic. Here, in the milky-coloured glacial river
called Portage Creek, one can see harlequin ducks feeding and displaying in the rushing water. Portage Glacier has in fact been receding
at a rate of around fifty feet per year for some years now, and in
another fifteen to twenty years will probably have backed out of the
lake which it excavated during its forward advance just over fifty years
ago. This lake, at present some two miles by one mile in extent,
reaches a depth of almost 600 feet in places. Before the lake existed, the

*Top* Except when forced lower
by snow, the mountain goat lives
at high elevations in the mountains around the Gulf of Alaska.

*Above* Although clearly visible in this picture, the female spruce grouse is protectively coloured with its barred and mottled plumage.

glacier provided a route between Cook Inlet and Prince William Sound for Tanaina Indians and others, and today it is followed by migratory birds, such as geese and cranes, during their spring and fall movements between Prince William Sound and western Alaska.

The Chugach Mountains have many of the same species of animals and flowers that have already been mentioned in connection with the Alaska Range and the Brooks Range. However, the southern slopes of the Chugach Mountains are the habitat of one animal not found in either of the main mountain ranges further north, and this is the mountain goat (*Oreamnos americanus*). From the south side of the Chugach Mountains this goat occurs in coastal mountains right down into The Panhandle, living almost entirely in rugged terrain above the timber line. The high ridges above Portage Creek are a good spot to look for the mountain goat. In the forests of the Chugach Mountains both the black bear and the moose can be seen frequently, as can the ridiculously tame spruce grouse (*Canachites canadensis*) which performs its courtship display on the forest floor.

Some of the alpine and sub-alpine meadows in the Chugach Mountains are really superb. I recall an area up above the Eagle River, near High Valley, which in mid-June was a mass of Kamchatka fritillaries, northern cranesbill and western columbine (*Aquilegia formosa*). Unlike the first two species the columbine does not occur in the Alaska Range, but it does extend round the Gulf of Alaska into The Panhandle. Above the south fork of the Eagle River is a side valley, the floor of which is about 2,700 feet above sea level. This valley is typical of many in the Chugach Mountains in July, yellow with lichens and a wonderful flora of dwarf birch and willow, Labrador tea, crowberry (*Empetrum nigrum*), cloudberry (*Rubus arcticus*), narcissus-flowered anemone (*Anemone narcissiflora*), Ross' avens (*Geum rossii*) and many others. The valley culminates in two cirques in the higher of which lies a nameless glacial lake, and on the high ridges round about, at 3,500 to 4,000 feet, are yet more flowers – mountain avens, diapensias, spotted saxifrages (*Saxifraga bronchialis*), wedge-leafed primroses and alpine arnicas. Here, too, are the characteristic alpine birds such as the water pipit, the horned lark and the gray-crowned rosy finch. At any time a bald eagle might pass overhead, for in the Chugach Mountains, particularly around the Gulf of Alaska, it is by no means an uncommon bird.

For more superb scenery and a wealth of wild flowers the area near Valdez is outstanding. Before reaching Valdez, the 'Little Switzerland' of Alaska, the Richardson Highway crosses the Chugach Mountains at Thompson Pass, at an altitude of very nearly 3,000 feet. This pass holds the Alaskan snowfall record of seventy-five feet and in winter it is as bleak and windswept as many places much further north. But what a contrast when summer comes and the slopes are covered with yellow mountain heather (*Phyllodoce aleutica*), forget-me-nots, saxifrages of various species, including prickly saxifrage (*Saxifraga tricuspidata*), Arctic harebells (*Campanula uniflora*) and rock jasmine (*Androsace chamaejasme*). Away down below to the south, weather permitting, the Lowe River can be seen as it disappears between the great rock walls of Keystone Canyon with its hanging waterfalls. Along the Richardson Highway in this part of the mountains the Sitka great burnet (*Sanguisorba stipulata*) may be found at the roadside, on stony slopes and in meadows bedstraw (*Galium boreale*) grows in profusion, and moist alpine situations will often produce the glaucous gentian (*Gentiana glauca*). From high slopes and ridges come the curious frog-like notes of rock ptarmigan, and looking eastwards one can see the snow-clad peaks of the Wrangell Mountains, sometimes called 'the jewels of central Alaska'.

# The Coasts and Islands

*There is a rapture on the lonely shore,*
*There is society, where none intrudes,*
*By the deep sea, and music in its roar.*

Byron

ONE of Alaska's greatest natural assets is her immense and varied tidal shoreline and numerous islands together with the vast array of wildlife associated with them. As was mentioned earlier, Alaska has nearly 35,000 miles of tidal shoreline which represents some thirty-eight per cent of the total tidal shoreline of the entire United States. In the north and west the shallow waters of the Chukchi and Bering Seas, which cover an enormous continental shelf area, extend up to 400 miles in width. For about nine degrees of latitude north of the Bering Strait the sea remains less than 100 fathoms deep. Off the north coast east of Point Barrow, the shelf area of the Arctic Ocean is much narrower. The shallow west coast waters contrast markedly with the immense depths of the Aleutian Trench, which lies immediately south of the Alaska Peninsula and the Aleutian Islands arc and reaches the incredible depth of 25,000 feet. This great trench with its associated island arc is the source of many of the earthquakes that occur in southern Alaska.

The Bering Sea is one of the continent's storm centres, for it is here that the relatively warm westerly winds sweeping up from the Pacific Ocean come face to face with the cold polar east winds from the mainland. Where they meet is the ever shifting boundary known as the polar front, and it is along this front that stormy areas of low pressure develop to more often than not roar off inland. The thunderous roar of great rollers is a characteristic sound of the Bering Sea coast where bad weather is regarded as more or less normal. Yet there can be days when the sea is calm and the sky blue, and then there is an atmosphere of great peace broken only by the whistle of shorebirds and the cries of white gulls winnowing overhead. Wind and rain are typical of the bleak Aleutian Islands as is evident from the stunted vegetation of a treeless landscape. Here they have winds known as 'williwaws', which can build up to gale force with quite unbelievable speed. It is a wind which sometimes even appears to be blowing straight up!

The desolate Aleutian Islands extend westwards for around 1,000 miles into the North Pacific close to the Asian mainland. Students of geography will find the Aleutians an intriguing place to study for they boast the most easterly point in the United States, as well as the most westerly. This may sound a complete contradiction, but Pochnoi Point on Semiscopochnoi Island lies just beyond the 180th meridian and is thus in the eastern hemisphere.

The polar sea ice clamps in to the coasts of the Arctic Ocean and the Bering Sea for almost two-thirds of the year, extending as far south as Bristol Bay. South of there and in the Gulf of Alaska the warm Alaska Current keeps the sea clear of ice, but sheltered areas such as Cook Inlet freeze over in winter. Spending winter in the Arctic, when there is hardly any difference in appearance between land and sea, must rate as one of life's great experiences. Gazing out from the north coast one sees an expanse of snow-covered ice, limitless in its extent, motionless, white and silent, sparkling beneath the northern sky and apparently lifeless. But this is the domain of the polar bear (*Ursus maritimus*), undoubtedly the most magnificent of the truly Arctic mammals, and more a marine than a land animal. The polar bear lives out its life on the pack ice often many miles from the nearest land, in a world of great pressure ridges and grinding ice and with no enemy but man. Occasionally polar bears come ashore in Alaska but rarely penetrate very far inland. However, in the fall of 1944 one was apparently killed some way inland on the Sagavanirktok River near the foothills of the Brooks Range.

The polar bear is found off the north Alaskan coast and, in winter, down the west coast sometimes as far south as St Lawrence Island south of the Bering Strait. They are most numerous on the southern edge of

*Preceding pages* Rugged cliffs look out across the storm-lashed waters of the Bering Sea on Alaska's west coast. *Inset* A group of emperor geese on the Bering Sea coast.

the pack ice and, therefore, those individuals that follow the ice south into the Bering Sea in winter, gradually shift north again round about April, keeping ahead of the retreating ice pack edge. Not infrequently these bears travel great distances on floating ice floes and some of these movements are doubtless involuntary. The appealing cubs are born in November or December in a den excavated in snow or ice. In other parts of its range the polar bear builds its den on large islands, but as Alaska does not have large islands off her north coast it must be assumed that the majority of dens there are in the offshore pack ice.

For what is technically a land mammal the polar bear is a superb swimmer: individuals have been seen swimming in the Arctic ocean fifty miles or more from the nearest ice. The main prey are seals such as the bearded (*Erignathus barbatus*), harbor (*Phoca vitulina*), ribbon (*Histriophoca fasciata*) and ringed (*Pusa hispida*) seals, all of which are associated with the Arctic pack ice. Despite its ability in the water the polar bear hunts seals primarily along the open leads where they congregate, either stalking them when they are hauled out on the ice,

A young harbor seal. Often young seals do not acquire their distinctive markings until the puppy fur is gone and they become sub-adult to full adult.

*Above left* The polar bear is the main predator in the world of the polar pack ice, where it preys extensively on seals.

*Left* In the Alaskan Panhandle many glaciers run down to the sea and they are the source of numerous icebergs.

*Above* Brown bear cubs on the Alaska Peninsula watch an adult fishing for salmon in the swirling waters of the rapids.

*Right* The northern or Steller's sea lion breeds on Bogoslof Island in the Aleutians.

*Overleaf* On Walrus Island in the Bering Sea up to 3,000 huge bull walruses may be hauled out on the beaches in summer.

or lying in ambush by a breathing hole. Carrion and birds' eggs are taken as opportunity offers.

How many polar bears there are in Alaska is not an easy question to answer as much still remains to be learnt despite the amount of research that has been done so far. In addition there is considerable movement over wide areas. A recent estimate by Thor Larsen of Oslo University puts the Alaskan and Canadian Arctic populations at about 2,500 and 6,000 respectively.

With the gradual rise in temperature as summer approaches, coupled with the effect of strong winds and currents, the ice parts from the shore and many open leads appear. Eventually the pack ice retreats away from the north coast a short distance and a narrow navigable channel is present for a few short weeks. Almost simultaneously with the movement away from shore of the ice comes the arrival of the summer populations of loons, ducks, geese, waders and gulls that were mentioned in an earlier chapter. They congregate first on any open leads in the sea ice, awaiting the opening up of the tundra pools. Occasionally large numbers of ducks such as eiders may arrive too soon; they find no open water and perhaps bad weather conditions, and at such times the resultant mortality can be tremendous.

In the Arctic Ocean, running more or less parallel with the mainland and only a short distance offshore, are a series of islands such as the Stockton Islands, Maguire Islands, McClure Islands, Midway Islands, Return Islands, and Jones Islands. Mostly they are barrier islands of gravel, long, narrow and low in profile. They provide sheltered water on the shoreward side and these sheltered stretches of sea are for a short while occupied by great rafts of ducks. I have for instance seen concentrations of oldsquaws or long-tailed ducks reaching 4,000 or more individuals. All the while other echelons are streaming overhead on their way east, a succession of formations of snow geese and black brants for example. Two miles out from shore off Prudhoe Bay I have also seen snowy and short-eared owls migrating eastwards across the ice.

Later the barrier islands are resorted to for nesting purposes by glaucous gulls and eider ducks. Occasionally one may find there the nest of the black brant, perhaps the most charming of the Arctic geese and one that appears to be unable to adapt to major changes in its chosen habitat. More nest on the mainland and during the flightless period in late summer these birds may be found concentrated in certain areas, such as the delta of the Kuparuk River. Two of the most handsome breeding species, the snow goose and Sabine's gull, must normally be looked for on islands in the river delta. A breeding colony of Sabine's gulls is an exciting place full of activity. These birds are a delight to watch, being so much more graceful than the larger glaucous gulls.

I am unlikely to forget my first visit to a breeding colony of snow geese. This did not take place until June 1971 when we located a colony on Howe Island. There were perhaps forty or fifty pairs of these geese nesting on the tundra of this moderate-sized island, and none had been breeding there in the two previous summers, or indeed anywhere else in the Prudhoe Bay area so far as we know. The nests were sited round the periphery of the island close to the sea, and all that I examined held a clutch of five eggs amongst a mass of soft white down. I also made the acquaintance of a strictly coastal flower. This was the Chukchi Sea primrose (*Primula borealis*) with pink or lilac petals and a yellow centre, that grows on saline shores along the north and west coasts of Alaska.

In the west of Alaska the long Bering Sea coast is so rich in wildlife that it justifies a book in itself. Through the Bering Strait and past

Point Barrow a vast migration of waterfowl passes in both spring and fall with eider ducks alone running into hundreds of thousands. The total number of all species involved in these migrations defeats the imagination for it comprises birds that not only nest in Alaska, but also in Siberia and Arctic Canada. If anything, perhaps the southward movements in the fall are even more impressive than those to the north in spring. In 1970, for instance, observers estimated that in an eight-week period from mid-July over 840,000 king eiders, common eiders, oldsquaws and black brants passed an observation post near Point Barrow, and these were only the ones that were actually seen.

As summer comes to the Bering Sea the northward retreat of the pack ice is followed by seals, the walrus (*Odobenus rosmarus*) and the beluga or white whale (*Delphinapterus leucos*), for it is not only birds that migrate north in the Arctic summer. When this season of migration is at hand and the ice is on the move, it is tremendously exciting to be off the Bering Sea coast watching what is happening out at sea. One may, for instance, see the sinuous co-ordinated grace of a school of killer whales (*Orcinus orca*) in pursuit of the belugas, their streamlined bodies slicing above the surface in unison and rolling below again. Then there may be heard the 'singing' of the walrus, a noise not unlike a distant band whose only instrument is a sort of banjo – I cannot think of anything else with which to compare the sound of the walrus. In an effort to frighten off enemies such as killer whales or polar bears they will trumpet loudly through the nostrils.

The walrus has been on the verge of extinction and even now is perhaps running close to the margin, for even though the Alaskan population may number about 95,000 animals the annual harvest is probably very near the reproduction rate. Reproduction is slow as the cows only bear one pup every two years. The Bering Sea offers many great sights, and among the more fantastic is a mass of bull walruses hauled out on the shores of Walrus Island, the only place in the United States where they come ashore. The huge bodies lie in tight formation and in every conceivable position. Squabbles break out and all the time there is much grunting, belching, snorting, wheezing and trumpeting. In fact the general impression is one of a horde of extremely obese and grossly over-fed men in the last stages of exhaustion. Around 3,000 bulls spend the year in and around this island.

Equally awe-inspiring is a visit to the islands of the seals, the usually mist- and fog-bound Pribilof Islands, 250 miles out to sea from the Aleutians. This is where the Alaskan fur seal (*Callorhinus alaskanus*) has its rookeries and harems, on the islands of St Paul and St George. How many fur seals? This is the first question that crosses the mind and the imagination boggles at the thought of trying to count them, but between one and a half and two million is not an unreasonable estimate. To all intents and purposes the scene is one of near total confusion and everlasting movement, not to mention noise. Bellowing bulls, and bawling litters of black pups, whose flippers are so large that one gets the impression that the body simply grew on as an afterthought, are on every hand. Animals are sprawled out in every direction and in every position with hind flippers waving in the air. The bulls in particular are rarely either still or quiet. Bellicosely defending their harems or fighting with other bulls, they are not animals to be taken lightly. A lunge at an opponent is accompanied by a violent burst of expelled breath and a cloud of spittle. The smell is as obvious as the noise and there is plenty of carrion to feed the multitudes of glaucous-winged gulls (*Larus glaucescens*) in attendance. The fur seal has a tight sleek coat with the astounding total of about 30,000 hairs to the square inch, an ideal adaptation for life in cold northern waters.

*Above* Once near the point of
extinction, the fur seal now has a
healthy population in the Bering
Sea. This is a four-year-old
bachelor.

*Left* With its large flippers, this
fur seal pup on the Pribilof
Islands has a very odd appearance.

The glaucous-winged gull is one of the abundant seabirds to be seen in the Gulf of Alaska.

One must be fair to the Pribilof Islands; they do have their balmy days of blue skies and brilliant sun, even if they are of rare occurrence. On such days one is almost surprised to find that there are meadows ablaze with yellow poppies and blue lupines (*Lupinus nootkatensis*). In fact many of the Bering Sea islands have lush vegetation in lowland areas, but this rapidly becomes sparse with increasing elevation and exposure.

When it comes to sheer numbers, then there is no question that it is the birds that dominate the scene. There is hardly an island in the Bering Sea or a mainland cliff that is not the site of vast seabird breeding colonies. The majority, if not all the islands in the Bering Sea, are of volcanic origin, and some of them formed part of the ancient Bering Land Bridge. Every ledge, crevice and pinnacle of the cliffs, every old crater and every volcanic ash bank is occupied by seabirds, and wherever there is a flat top it will more likely than not be packed with ranks of common murres or guillemots (*Uria aalge*) or thick-billed murres (*Uria lomvia*). The sea around these islands is a mass of birds diving, surfacing, floating in great rafts or swimming in long lines. As the boat approaches the precipitous cliffs one hears the remarkable 'murmuration' produced by thousands upon thousands of birds on the ledges. Any sudden panic that hits these colonies results in a roar of massed wings like the sound of a gale through a forest canopy.

The question of numbers becomes somewhat academic in such circumstances. Who can objectively try to compute statistics when confronted for the first time with one of the great natural sights of the world? Colonies of hundreds of thousands can be considered normal. The fulmar (*Fulmarus glacialis*), for instance, has some colossal colonies in the Bering Sea. On the island of St Matthew one colony alone extends along at least five miles of cliff. On the ledges of St Paul there are probably one and a half million murres packed in at nesting time. About 250 miles north of St Matthew is the large island of St Lawrence where the numbers of crested auklets (*Aethia cristatella*) and least auklets (*A. pusilla*) present in summer have been estimated respectively at about one and a half million and almost one million. These totals include non-breeding as well as breeding birds. But even the numbers involved for the breeding colonies almost pale into significance compared with those attained by a non-breeding visitor to Alaskan waters. This is the slender-billed shearwater (*Puffinus tenuirostris*) which breeds in Australian waters but comes to the Bering Sea in the course of its migrations, and is most numerous there from June to September. The place to see these shearwaters at their best is in Unimak Pass in the Aleutians, and their numbers can be assessed in millions. One great naturalist, Ira Gabrielson, described this annual migration of shearwaters along the Alaskan coast as the 'greatest panorama of life on the North American continent'.

Some miles south-west of Unimak Pass lies Bogoslof Island whose birth was typical of the violent geological history of the Aleutians. Bogoslof Island, it is recorded, rose from the cold waters about 175 years ago with a sound like thunder, a flame from the sea and a jolting earthquake. Here may be seen colonies of murres along with both horned puffins (*Fratercula corniculata*) and tufted puffins (*Lunda cirrhata*), but the numbers do not match those that occur elsewhere in the Bering Sea. Also found on Bogoslof Island is the northern or Steller's sea lion (*Eumetopias jubata*). It breeds on the island where its numbers may sometimes exceed 5,000.

Most of the Bering Sea islands are remote and this fact, coupled with the formidable combination of frequent fog, gales and violent seas, means that opportunities to visit most of them even in summer are few. This is perhaps just as well for it is imperative that the huge assemblies of seabirds and mammals be preserved for posterity. In a world of rapidly decreasing wilderness and wildlife, the islands of this Arctic sea stand unique. Many of the islands are included in the national wildlife refuge system. St Matthew, Hall and Pinnacle Islands in the north-central Bering Sea form the Bering Sea National Wildlife Refuge, while most of the Aleutian arc is in the Aleutian Islands National Wildlife Refuge. In Kotzebue Sound the Chamisso National Wildlife Refuge comprising Chamisso and Puffin Islands and the adjacent islets, is one of the most important breeding areas for seabirds on the north-west coast of Alaska. Between Bristol Bay and the Kuskokwim Delta the steep cliffs of the Cape Newenham National Wildlife Refuge support one of the largest nesting colonies of seabirds in North America, with over a million puffins, murres and blacklegged kittiwakes (*Rissa tridactyla*). It is to be hoped that these refuges will survive the inevitable pressures of coming decades, but after the way in which the Atomic Energy Commission was allowed to detonate nuclear devices on Amchitka in the Aleutians in 1971, one can be forgiven for feeling a certain degree of scepticism.

It is among the kelp beds of the Aleutians that the sea otter, once on the verge of extinction, has been nursed back to a healthy population. Nevertheless, even now, it has probably recolonized barely one-fifth of its original range. It is likely in any event that much of the former range could no longer support sea otters due to pollution and other factors. Like the walrus, reproduction is slow with breeding taking place only every other year. There can be few more remarkable animals in the world than the sea otter. It is one of the few mammals other than man which has learnt the use of tools. It feeds mainly on crabs, clams, fishes and sea urchins, consuming something like a quarter of its own weight in food each day. Floating on its back it breaks open the shellfish, which are held in the front paws, against a flat stone on its chest. The sea otter in fact spends its life almost entirely on its back; it sleeps in that position and the young are carried around on the female's chest. It is to Alaska that one can now go to enjoy the charming spectacle of sea

otters floating on their backs in the translucent water of the kelp beds, a wonderful sight that represents a victory for scientific conservation.

From the Aleutians round to Prince William Sound the sea otter population now numbers perhaps a little in excess of 30,000 animals. One of the numerous interesting aspects of their biology is that, unlike other marine mammals, they do not have a layer of insulating blubber but rely for insulation upon air trapped in the fine, dense fur. The sea otter is, therefore, constantly working on its fur, preening and grooming every part of the body. In fact it can be said that at any given time a sea otter, if not feeding or sleeping, will be grooming itself. This is hardly surprising since its life depends upon maintaining the insulating qualities of the fur.

*Above* A female sea otter clasps her young to her chest.

*Right* In the vast delta area of the Yukon River a sandhill crane prepares to settle on its eggs.

A complete contrast to the rugged volcanic islands of the Bering Sea is provided by the vast level areas of marshy tundra forming the river delta areas of the west coast. Here are some of the most important wader- and waterfowl-producing areas in Alaska. It has been estimated, for instance, that from the Yukon Delta alone some two million waterfowl leave each fall for the south. The deltas of the Yukon and Kuskokwim Rivers form one huge area that I first visited in June 1969. I went to Igiak Bay which is part of the 1.8 million acre Clarence Rhode National Wildlife Range. We flew from Anchorage to Bethel by commercial airline, but the remainder of the journey was completed by Cessna 180 floatplane piloted by Calvin Lensink, Refuge Manager. On the way to Igiak Bay we stopped off at the abandoned Eskimo village of Old Chevak on the Kashunuk River where there is a field station. The tundra was alive with birds including whistling swans, sandhill cranes, Sabine's gulls, Arctic terns, long-billed dowitchers, old-squaws, greater scaups, long-tailed jaegers and western sandpipers (*Ereunetes mauri*). It was rather overwhelming.

Here occurred one of those frustrating experiences with which all ornithologists are familiar. Flying across the tundra beyond the river were two largish waders with decurved bills and what appeared to be tawny-coloured rump and tail, but they came and went so quickly. Did we really hear what sounded suspiciously like a 'wolf whistle'? Were they in fact bristle-thighed curlews (*Numenius tahitiensis*) or were we

A white-fronted goose approaches its nest on the grassy tundra of the Bering Sea coast.

indulging in wishful thinking? Unfortunately the distance was great and the view fleeting, and now we shall never know. This rare curlew whose nest and eggs defied discovery until 1948, when two nests were found on the barren tundra near the lower Yukon River, is believed to breed in the low ranges between the Kuskokwim and Yukon Rivers, and occurs on the coastal tundra of the Clarence Rhode National Wildlife Range.

This disappointment was soon forgotten as we flew on low over lake-studded grassy tundra to Igiak Bay. As the Bering Sea came into view we dropped down to a perfect landing on one of the multitude of lakes. The main reason for my wanting to visit this remote delta area, was the emperor goose (*Philacte canagica*), for here a very large propor-tion of the Alaskan population of the species breeds. (The Yukon Delta, in fact, produces ninety per cent of the world's emperor geese.) Sure enough within an hour or so we had found nearly two dozen nests, some still containing eggs. This beautiful silvery-grey goose has a white head and neck (normally stained a rusty shade by iron oxides in the water) which makes it, at least so I thought, rather obvious when it is sitting on the nest. It was very difficult to concentrate on any one thing due to the abundant birdlife on every hand for, in addition to emperor geese, there were numerous nesting black brants, white-fronted geese, oldsquaws, spectacled eiders (*Lampronetta fischeri*), greater scaups and green-winged teals. It was becoming too much. I could not write notes fast enough to keep up with what was happening to us, and on top of it all I was at one stage mobbed by two pairs of Sabine's gulls concerned about their nearby nests. In addition to the waterfowl, there were sandhill cranes who proved much more wary than the geese when it came to finding their nest. Waders too were present in great numbers including such familiar species as dunlin and bar-tailed godwit (*Limosa*

The eggs of this female spectacled eider are well protected from cold winds off the stormy Bering Sea.

*lapponica*), and oh how red those godwits were in the bright Arctic sun. An entirely new wader to me was the black turnstone (*Arenaria melanocephala*) which was quite common. Just offshore from this wildlife range is the Hazen Bay National Wildlife Refuge which consists of the islands of Kigigak and Nunivakchak, a concentrated nesting area for the black brant and other species.

The deltas are staging as well as producing areas and migrant waterfowl in colossal numbers use them for varying periods. Through the Yukon Delta area pass great congregations of snow geese on their way to nesting areas in Siberia, Arctic Alaska and Canada. Further south, on the Alaska Peninsula, what might well be classed as some of the most stupendous concentrations of wild geese in the world occur in Izembek Bay, where extensive eelgrass beds provide a rich source of food. It is an amazing place, one day in the fall there may be barely a handful of geese, but the following day might see the arrival of as many as 20,000 in one flight alone. For two or three months each year virtually the entire black brant population of the North American continent will be gathered in Izembek Bay, and it is quite likely that the area is essential to the survival of the species. All the Alaskan and probably most of the Siberian populations of emperor geese also pass through Izembek Bay. At times the bay may hold 300,000 geese and even more ducks.

When we leave the Bering Sea and cross the Alaska Peninsula to the Gulf of Alaska we enter a rather different world, but one which has its own wonders. The thirty-mile-wide Shelikof Strait separates Kodiak Island from the peninsula, and this island is the home of the largest living terrestial carnivore in the world. This is the Kodiak brown bear. A really big male may tip the scales at 2,200 pounds and stand a little over nine feet in height when up on his back legs. According to a recent estimate by Mctaggart Cowan, the present population of these bears on Kodiak Island is about 3,300 which means that there is almost one bear per square mile, Kodiak Island being 3,500 square miles in extent. Some of the deep trails worn by the constant passage of these huge bears can be seen from a very considerable height when flying over the island. Despite their enormous size and notwithstanding numerous stories to the contrary, the Kodiak brown bear is basically adverse to confrontations with human beings.

The best time to see these bears is in July and August when they congregate to feed on the abundant salmon making their way upriver to the spawning grounds. The best fishing spots are the province of the older and dominant bears; the younger animals have to make do with second best. It is interesting to see how much time and energy young bears waste in the process of learning the art of fishing. As a matter of interest, I believe that the majority of fishes are caught in the jaws and not scooped out with a swipe of the paw as has been said in various articles and books. I think, also, that it is spawned-out salmon that forms the bulk of their catch.

Another of the impressive sights of Kodiak Island is the majestic flight of the bald eagle. Indeed there is hardly a moment when one of these fine birds is not in view. It has been estimated that perhaps 200 pairs breed on the island. It is also worth mentioning that there are elk (*Cervus canadensis*) on Afognak and Raspberry Islands near Kodiak. Personally I find it difficult to get enthusiastic about them as they were transplanted there from the Olympic Peninsula in Washington state some years ago. Not even the fact that elk roamed the Alaskan interior in the Pleistocene can alter this feeling about their introduced presence now.

In July and August by the falls on the McNeil River, just north of Cape Douglas on the Alaska Peninsula, one can see the greatest known concentration of brown bears in the world. Sixty or more gather to take advantage of the spawning run of salmon up the river. Such a concentration is all the more remarkable when we remember that this brown bear is not normally a gregarious animal, but of course these gatherings last only for a few weeks.

Even the concentration of bald eagles on Kodiak Island can be surpassed if we cross the gulf to Admiralty Island, close to Juneau in the matchless coastal scenery of The Panhandle. This island, perhaps about half the size of Kodiak Island and with a spine of mountains rising to 4,639 feet, was estimated, in 1966, to have no less than 443 bald eagle nests. It also boasts a very substantial population of the giant brown bears, perhaps in excess of 1,000 animals. Besides this wealth of wild-life, the island is endowed with breathtaking scenery and isolation.

Further north in The Panhandle, at Yakutat Bay, it is still possible to see a rare colour form of the black bear that is known locally as the glacier bear. The animal, which is a pale bluish-grey in colour, comes as something of a surprise to those who think that all black bears must be black, which of course is not the case. The glacier bear has inevitably had a thin time with hunters due to its rarity value.

When it comes to birds, the Gulf of Alaska can rival the Bering Sea coast in the numbers of seabirds, shorebirds and waterfowl to be seen there, particularly at migration time. Many of the largest colonies of breeding seabirds are on the west side of the gulf. On Chisik Island, which rises massively from the sea to a height of 2,600 feet, there is a black-legged kittiwake colony, some two miles long, which has been estimated to contain about 45,000 birds. The kittiwake is but one of seven species that occur in the northern gulf in numbers that have to be assessed in millions. The other species are the sooty shearwater (*Puffinus griseus*) and the western sandpiper, both of which occur as migrants only, and the fork-tailed petrel (*Oceanodroma furcata*), pintail, northern phalarope, and common murre, all of which breed as well as migrate through the area. There is a breeding colony of about 10,000 fork-tailed petrels on the Barren Islands.

One of the least known breeding species of the Gulf of Alaska is the marbled murrelet (*Brachyramphus marmoratum*) whose population probably exceeds 50,000 birds and which is suspected of nesting above the timberline on coastal mountains and islands. In the Copper River delta area almost the entire North American population (numbering over 35,000 birds) of a race of the Canada goose known as the dusky Canada goose (*Branta canadensis occidentalis*) breeds. Nowhere else in the United States is it possible to see such numbers of bald eagles. In addition to the numbers on Admiralty Island that I mentioned earlier, it has been estimated that about 700 pairs nest around the north coast of the Gulf of Alaska. In late September and October the total number of bald eagles present in the northern gulf (excluding Prince William Sound) may exceed 10,000 birds. Late spawning salmon at Cordova in December 1969 attracted a gathering of 416 bald eagles.

But for the really huge numbers of birds it is the migration seasons that produce the goods. Areas such as the Susitna Flats in the west and the Copper River delta in the east are simply alive with shore-birds and waterfowl. In the latter area it has been calculated that from late April through to mid-May the 200 or more square miles of mud flats are utilized by something like twenty million shorebirds, ducks and geese. Equivalent numbers of some species appear also in the fall, and a five-day period in late September one year saw more than 500,000 sandhill cranes pass through the delta area. Seabirds too swarm on migration, and as an example one can quote the estimated minimum of 2·6 million sooty shearwaters seen off the Barren Islands in June 1965.

It must be very difficult for anyone who has not seen these incredible numbers of birds against the sheer beauty of the wild scenery of the Gulf of Alaska, to realize what a wonderful experience it is – a visual experience that is heightened by the multitudinous excited calls of these millions of birds gathered at one of the great migration crossroads of the world. Yet on a smaller scale and in a different form there are many other beautiful sights to be seen around the Gulf of Alaska. The road from Anchorage to Palmer, for example, passes the Eklutna Flats, an area of saline meadows by Cook Inlet. Here, in summer, there is a veritable blaze of mixed colours formed by millions of blooms of shooting stars, Kamchatka fritillaries and wild flags (*Iris setosa*).

On a totally different plane, who could fail to be impressed, or indeed overawed, by the hostile and icy splendour of the 3,554 square miles of the Glacier Bay National Monument just to the south of Yakutat Bay. Glacier Bay itself now consists of some fifty miles of open water, but 250 years ago it was solid ice. From high in the towering mountains round the bay, rivers of ice grind down into eight fiord-like inlets. In such surroundings man is a nonentity.

124

In the fall, when salmon ascend
the rivers to spawn, brown
bears become almost exclusively
fish-eaters.

# Index

Page numbers in italic refer to illustrations

# Acknowledgements

**Colour** British Petroleum Co. Ltd. 15(top), 26–27; Bruce Coleman Ltd. – Sven Gillsater 110(top), Leonard Lee Rue 82(bottom right inset), James Simon 58, Joe Van Wormer 79, 87, 111(bottom); J. Faro 106(inset), 110–111; Pete Martin 6–7, 14–15, 18–19, 27, 90–91, 95, 110(bottom); Steve McCutcheon 74–75, 106–107; D. H. Pimlott 70; Bryan Sage front jacket, 2–3, 10–11, 15(bottom), 19(top), 19(bottom), 22–23, 30–31, 50(top), 50(centre), 50(bottom), 54–55, 54(inset), 55(inset), 58–59, 59(top), 59(bottom), 62(top), 62(bottom left), 62(bottom right), 63(top left), 63(top right), 63 (bottom), 71, 78, 82–83, 82(bottom left inset), 86(left), 86(right), 94(top), 94(bottom), 98–99, 99(top), 99(bottom), 102(left), 102–103, 102(right), 103(left), back jacket; W. Stribling 51 (bottom), 66–67, 103(right); Michael Wotton 51(top).
**Black and white** Alaska Department of Fish and Game 118–119; Bruce Coleman Ltd. – Sven Gillsater 33, Russ Kinne 34, Charlie Ott 44, Leonard Lee Rue 77(bottom); Eric Hosking 120; Jerry L. Hout 68–69, 69; Steve McCutcheon 109, 113, 115(top), 115(bottom), 124–125; Charlie Ott 40, 72–73, 81(top), 81(bottom); D. H. Pimlott 9, 47; Bryan Sage 24–25, 41, 42–43, 56, 57, 88–89, 116; W. Stribling 38, 61, 77(top), 96, 104–105(top), 104–105(bottom); Michael Wotton 119, 121.

The publishers are grateful to Dodd, Mead & Company, McGraw-Hill Ryerson Limited and Ernest Benn Limited for permission to reprint extracts from *The Collected Poems of Robert Service*, and to Robert Weeden for permission to quote from a paper entitled *Man in Nature: a Strategy for Alaskan Living* published in *Productivity and Conservation in Northern Circumpolar Lands*, I.U.C.N. 1970.